Dietrich Bonhoeffer

Dietrich Bonhoeffer
A Life in Pictures

Centenary Edition

Edited by Renate Bethge
and Christian Gremmels

Translator – Brian McNeil
Editorial Consultant – Holger Sweers
Layout – Holger Lindner

Fortress Press
Minneapolis

DIETRICH BONHOEFFER
A Life in Pictures

Centenary edition published by Fortress Press in 2006.

Translated by Brian McNeil from the German *Dietrich Bonhoeffer: Bilder eines Lebens*, copyright © 2005, by Gütersloher Verlagshaus, Gütersloh, and copyright © 1986 Christian Kaiser Verlag, Munich, Germany.

Editorial consultant: Holger Sweers
Layout: Holger Lindner

ISBN 0-8006-3811-5

Manufactured in Germany

09 08 07 06   1   2   3   4   5   6   7

Foreword

The scene is New York, in the spring of 2004. The photographer André Lutzen has made a life-size figure of Dietrich Bonhoeffer, and is walking with it through the streets of Manhattan. Several people call out to him: "Surely that's Bonhoeffer!" They recognize him because the figure is modeled on what is probably the best known photograph of Dietrich Bonhoeffer, taken in the summer of 1944. It shows him as a prisoner in the courtyard of the Military Prison for those awaiting trial, in Berlin-Tegel.

Sixty years lie between that photograph in Tegel and its presentation in New York. In this period, thanks to the publication of Bonhoeffer's writings by Eberhard Bethge, his theological influence has spread throughout the world. But he is also present in images, in a manner unique among the theologians of the century in which he lived: his theological work which is bound to the *word*, and the story of his life which is portrayed in the *image*, form a synthesis.

We owe our thanks to the Bonhoeffer family for making this second element a possibility. They began at a very early date to send photographs of their children, from babyhood to adolescence, to their far-flung relatives. Occasionally, professional photographers came to the house, so that the pictures would satisfy the most exacting demands: no artificial "photographed faces," and of course a bodily posture, haircut, and clothes that were neither too stiff nor too loose. In the 1920s, photographs were taken by the younger children as they tried out their new cameras in the garden and on excursions. Dietrich Bonhoeffer's papers include the negatives of photographs he took on his travels in Libya, Spain, and Mexico. When he began his professional work, he had very little time for taking photographs; but then his students began to sense that it was important to have a visual record of their teacher, and many snapshots were taken. We also have the group photographs of the candidates in all the courses at the Finkenwalde seminary and of those who took part in the "collective vicariates" in Gross-Schlönwitz, Köslin, and Sigurdshof. No professional photographers took pictures of Bonhoeffer himself: one made portraits of high ecclesiastical office-bearers, not of a young man who led an illegal existence. Picture postcards of Martin Niemöller and Hans Asmussen circulated at that time in the Confessing Church — but not of Bonhoeffer. In the last stage of his life, a master sergeant in the guard battalion in Tegel brought his camera to work, so that he could take pictures of some of the inmates — and of himself in the center of their group — as if he was just a little proud of his prisoners. Perhaps he believed that his job was drawing to its close.

We can see all of this, but there are other areas of Bonhoeffer's life which are not recorded in photographs. We have no pictures of the family's musical life, neither of the trios in the Wangenheimstraße nor of the family's quartets and cantatas in the Marienburger Allee 42. There is no photograph that shows Dietrich Bonhoeffer with his fiancée, Maria von Wedemeyer. No photograph shows the interior of his cell in Tegel, and this is even more true of the next stations along the path he took from the Gestapo dungeon in the Prinz-Albrecht-Straße via Buchenwald to the concentration camp at Flossenbürg.

The pictures in this book and the short accompanying texts give a vivid first impression of Bonhoeffer's life and work. To learn more, one can usefully see the edition of his writings in sixteen volumes; and a most helpful book is by Eberhard Bethge, *Dietrich Bonhoeffer: A Biography* (revised edition, Minneapolis: Fortress Press, 2000).

The private world of his family, the individual path of his life, and his writings, which remained only fragmentary — in the aftermath of his early death in Flossenbürg, these have become an inheritance that has given many Christians strength and courage. When we experience something of this inheritance in the present book, our eyes are opened to perceive a theological achievement which is not yet fully understood. Nor have its implications been put into practice. That task still lies ahead of us!

Renate Bethge and Christian Gremmels
Wachtberg and Reinhardshagen
April 9, 2005

Contents

Family background

Cultivating a great inheritance

The world of his ancestors provided Dietrich Bonhoeffer with the standards he followed in his own life. The sureness of judgment, the confidence when he spoke in public – those could not be acquired in one single generation. He inherited them from his ancestors. He grew up in a family which held that the truest educational input came not from a school, but from a deeply rooted obligation to cultivate a great historical inheritance with its intellectual traditions. In Dietrich Bonhoeffer's case, this meant learning to understand and respect what other people had thought and experienced before him. And this could mean that he must make his own contribution in such a way that he would honor his ancestors precisely by making a decision on some substantial issue that was the opposite of theirs!

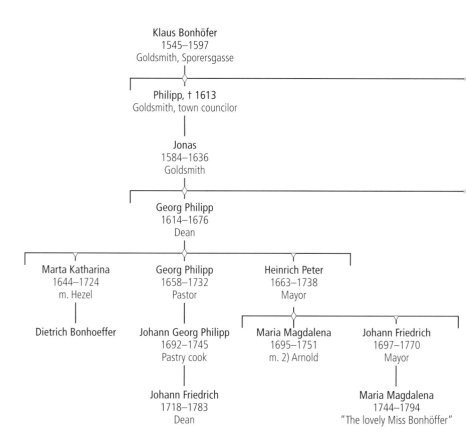

Klaus Bonhöfer
1545–1597
Goldsmith, Sporersgasse

Philipp, † 1613
Goldsmith, town councilor

Jonas
1584–1636
Goldsmith

Georg Philipp
1614–1676
Dean

Marta Katharina
1644–1724
m. Hezel

Georg Philipp
1658–1732
Pastor

Heinrich Peter
1663–1738
Mayor

Dietrich Bonhoeffer

Johann Georg Philipp
1692–1745
Pastry cook

Maria Magdalena
1695–1751
m. 2) Arnold

Johann Friedrich
1697–1770
Mayor

Johann Friedrich
1718–1783
Dean

Maria Magdalena
1744–1794
"The lovely Miss Bonhöffer"

The preacher Georg Philipp Bonhöfer (1614-1676) with his two wives, Anna Marie Müller (1621-1649) and Eufrosine Katharine Gräter (1631-1703).
St. Michael in Schwäbisch Hall.

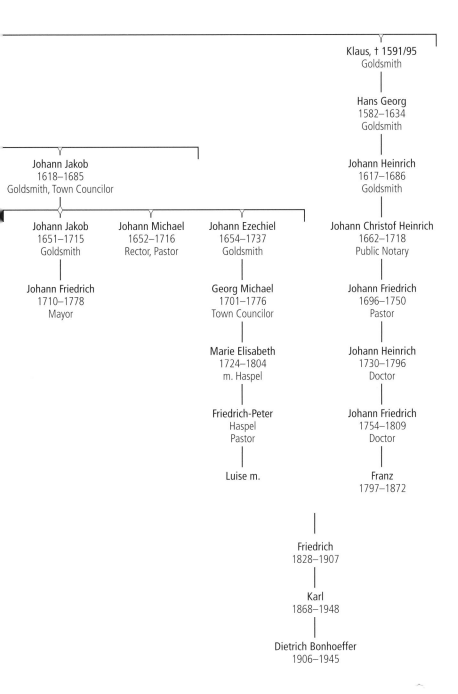

Klaus, † 1591/95
Goldsmith

Hans Georg
1582–1634
Goldsmith

Johann Heinrich
1617–1686
Goldsmith

Johann Jakob
1618–1685
Goldsmith, Town Councilor

Johann Christof Heinrich
1662–1718
Public Notary

Johann Jakob
1651–1715
Goldsmith

Johann Michael
1652–1716
Rector, Pastor

Johann Ezechiel
1654–1737
Goldsmith

Johann Friedrich
1710–1778
Mayor

Georg Michael
1701–1776
Town Councilor

Johann Friedrich
1696–1750
Pastor

Marie Elisabeth
1724–1804
m. Haspel

Johann Heinrich
1730–1796
Doctor

Friedrich-Peter
Haspel
Pastor

Johann Friedrich
1754–1809
Doctor

Luise m.

Franz
1797–1872

Friedrich
1828–1907

Karl
1868–1948

Dietrich Bonhoeffer
1906–1945

above:
Johann Friedrich Bonhöffer (1718–1783), Dean.

below:
Maria Magdalena Bonhöffer (1744–1794),
the "lovely Miss Bonhöffer."

Epitaphs, St. Michael, Schwäbisch Hall.

On his father's side

The family van den Boenhoff immigrated from Nijmegen in Holland and worked as goldsmiths in Schwäbisch Hall from the sixteenth century on. In the following century, they became pastors, doctors, town councilors, and mayors.

Thanks to the marriage of his grandfather, Friedrich Bonhoeffer (1828-1907), with Julie Tafel (1842-1936), Dietrich's ancestors included a revolutionary element: Julie's father Friedrich and his brother Gottlob were temporarily banished from Württemberg because they belonged to student fraternities and had democratic ideas. Gottlob was imprisoned in Hohenasperg in 1824.

above:
The Bonhoeffer coat of arms with a lion holding a bean-plant in its paws (Klosterstr. 7, Schwäbisch Hall).

below:
The "Table brothers", known (from the left) as the "wise," the "wild," the "pious," and the "hand-some Table." A contemporary engraving in the study of Dietrich Bonhoeffer's father.

above:
Grandfather Friedrich
Bonhoeffer (1828–1907),
ca. 1900.

below:
Grandmother Julie
Bonhoeffer (1842–1936),
1932.

Dietrich knew his grandfather, who was president of the circuit court in Ulm, only by hearsay, but his grandmother survived long into his own lifetime. On her 90th birthday in 1932, a little poem was written for all her great-grandchildren to recite: "When you were as small as I am now, people rode on horses. When I am as old as you are now, people will be shot to the Moon in rockets." One year later, at the age of 91, she ignored the SA cordon which demonstrated in front of the "Western Store" in Berlin, demanding a boycott of Jewish businesses. Julie Bonhoeffer died at the beginning of January, 1936. Dietrich Bonhoeffer preached at her burial, and his words contained a promise:

"Our years are three score and ten, or even by reason of strength fourscore. And even if it was delightful, yet it was work and toil." She lived to be 93, and she transmitted to us the inheritance of another time. With her, a world that we all somehow bear in ourselves – and indeed wish to bear in ourselves – sinks down out of our sight. With all her heart, she believed in the universal validity of the law, in the free word of the free man, in the binding character of a promise once given, in clarity and sobriety of speech, in honesty and moderation in private and public life. That was the world in which she lived. In her own life, she learned that it costs work and toil to realize these goals in one's own life. She did not disdain this work and toil. She found it intolerable to see that other people scorned these goals, and human rights were crushed under foot. This is why her last years were saddened by the terrible suffering caused her by what is happening to the Jews among our people. She bore this suffering too, she suffered along with them. She came from another time, from another world of the spirit – and this world does not sink down with her into the grave. This inheritance, for which we are grateful to her, imposes an obligation on us.

On his mother's side

Count Stanislaus von Kalckreuth (1820-1894), Dietrich's great-grandfather, abandoned the profession of his ancestors – a military career and huge landed estates – to take up painting. His son, Leopold von Kalckreuth, was an even better painter than his father. Two of their paintings hang in Dietrich's study in the Marienburger Allee, where he was arrested in 1943.

The Kalckreuth family embodied the Prussian world in miniature. The wedding of Clara von Kalckreuth (1851-1903), Dietrich's grandmother, with Karl Alfred von Hase (1842-1914) was celebrated in 1871 in Weimar as a double wedding; on the same occasion, her older sister Anna married Count Hans Yorck von Wartenburg, who lived on the estate of Klein-Oels in Silesia. This great-aunt was much loved by the Bonhoeffer children later on. She invited them to Klein-Oels and often came to visit them. Clara's sister Pauline became a lady-in-waiting to Crown Princess Victoria, the wife of Frederick III, in Potsdam.

After the war with France (1870-1871), Karl Alfred von Hase became a military chaplain in Hanover, and was later appointed chief military chaplain in Königsberg, where his daughter Paula – Dietrich's mother – was born in 1876. In 1889, Karl Alfred von Hase was appointed court preacher in Potsdam by Wilhelm II, but he asked to be released from this position two and a half years later. In 1894, he became consistorial counselor and professor of practical theology in Breslau.

above:
Great-grandfather Kalckreuth with his daughters Clara, Pauline, and Helene.

below:
Clara von Hase with her husband Karl Alfred von Hase and her sister Helene Yorck von Wartenburg.

Dietrich Bonhoeffer's grandfather cherished the memory of his more famous father, Karl August von Hase (1800-1890), professor of church and dogmatic history in Jena. He was expelled from Leipzig and Erlangen because of his membership in a student fraternity, and he began his academic career in Tübingen, until the authorities expelled him from that town too and kept him in prison in Hohenasperg for more than a year (1824-1825). In 1831, Karl August von Hase married Pauline Härtel, the daughter of a Leipzig publisher. His textbook on the history of dogma was still prized by students in Bonhoeffer's day as an aid in preparing for examinations.

left:
Karl August von Hase.

below left:
Karl Alfred von Hase.

below right:
Clara von Hase
shortly after her marriage.

His parents

As a young woman, Dietrich Bonhoeffer's mother persuaded her parents to allow her to study to become a teacher. In April, 1894, she received her diploma as a teacher in "intermediary and higher girls' schools." The family used to say later on that she had remarked that Germans had their backbone broken twice in life: once in school, then during military service. Is this perhaps why she herself taught her children in the first years of their life?

In 1893, just after taking his doctorate, Karl Bonhoeffer left Tübingen and took up the post of assistant to Carl Wernicke, the leading German professor of psychiatry, in Breslau. Three years later, in the house of the physicist Otto Meyer, he met "a young blond, blue-eyed girl who cast such a spell on me as soon as she entered the room, thanks to her free, natural posture and the open and uninhibited way she looked at me, that this moment in which I met for the first time the woman who was to become my wife remains in my memory as an almost mystical impression which was decisive for the whole course of my life" (from his memoirs).

Diploma of the Royal Provincial School College in Breslau for Miss Paula von Hase.

above:

Karl and Paula Bonhoeffer shortly after their marriage in Breslau.

below:

Paula von Hase.

Karl Bonhoeffer as a medical student in Tübingen (front row, middle).

Childhood and Youth
(1906–23)

Birkenwäldchen 7 in Breslau

Dietrich's father began his career as university teacher and director of a clinic in Breslau, the capital of Silesia. This was also the place where the children had their earliest experiences and made their first discoveries. Their father wrote: "We had the good fortune to have a pretty and spacious house set in a large garden in Birkenwäldchen, near the clinics, and this gave the children a great freedom of movement. The garden with its old trees had not been properly looked after. In winter, we poured water on an old tennis court with an asphalt surface, so that the two oldest children could try skating for the first time. We had a big outbuilding meant to hold a carriage. We didn't have a carriage or horses, but we did use this outbuilding to keep all kinds of animals. The apartment of grandfather Hase and aunt Elisabeth was opposite our house on the other bank of the arm of the river Oder, so that we often went from one house to the other."

above:
Paula Bonhoeffer with her children in the garden.

below:
Breslau, Birkenwäldchen 7.

Karl-Friedrich (1899–1957)

Walter (1899–1918)

Klaus (1901–1945)

Ursula (1902–1983)

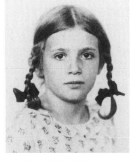

Christine (1903–1965)

Dietrich (1906–1945)

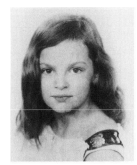

Sabine (1906–1999)

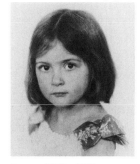

Susanne (1909–1991)

(Photographs ca. 1913)

Brothers and sisters

On February 4, 1906, the twins Dietrich and Sabine were born in Breslau, the sixth and seventh children of Karl and Paula Bonhoeffer. In 1909, the youngest sister, Susanne, was born. On New Year's Eve 1909, Karl Bonhoeffer wrote in his diary for December 31: "Despite having eight children – which seems an enormous number in times like these – we have the impression that there are not too many of them! The house is big, the children develop normally, we parents are not too old, and so we endeavor not to spoil them, and to make their young years enjoyable."

The twins Dietrich and Sabine, 1914.

left:
Paula Bonhoeffer with her eight children.

A carefree childhood

The parents did not send their children to the children's service in church. For baptisms etc., they had recourse to clergymen who were members of the family – first to the children's grandfather, then to the mother's brother, Hans von Hase. The group of children were particularly fond of playing at "baptism."

In view of the rapidly increasing number of their children, the parents began to look for a suitable place for holidays. In 1910, they found a house in the Glatz mountains, near the Bohemian border, two hours by train from Breslau.

Their father paints a vivid picture of Wölfelsgrund in his memoirs: the holiday house lay "in a little valley at the foot of Mount Urnitz, right at the edge of the wood, with a meadow, a little brook, an old barn, and a fruit-tree which had a raised seat with a little bench for the children built into its wide branches."

above:
Wölfelsgrund, July 1911.

below left:
The baptism of the youngest sister, Susanne, by her grandfather, Karl Alfred von Hase, 1909. The twins Dietrich and Sabine are in the front row.

below right:
The children play at baptism.

In 1912, the father was appointed professor at the Friedrich Wilhelm University in Berlin. As director of the university neurological clinic, the Charité, he held the leading professorial chair for psychology and neurology in Germany. The family lived first in the Brückenallee near the Bellevue railway station, where the professors at the Charité lived at that time.

After Sunday supper, their father sometimes read aloud to the assembled family, which also included Maria Horn, the governess of the Bonhoeffer children:

He read letters of Fontaine and Dostoevsky's "Letters from the Underworld." He also read Schiller's writings, "Those who see ghosts," "Criminals from a lost marriage," and even "Grace and Dignity," which I unfortunately found boring. He also took the trouble to make us acquainted with Fritz Reuter and read "Ut mine Stromtid" to us, doing his best to speak the dialect (Susanne Dress, Bonhoeffer's youngest sister).

From the fall of 1913 to the spring of 1919, Dietrich Bonhoeffer attended the Friedrich-Werder Grammar School in Berlin.

above:
An evening spent reading, ca. 1913.

center:
Dietrich Bonhoeffer (second row from bottom, third from left) with his classmates.

Maria Horn.

Friedrichsbrunn

After the move to Berlin, the holiday house in Wölfelsgrund was too far away, so they had to sell it. In 1913, the Bonhoeffers bought a former forester's house in Friedrichsbrunn, a health resort in the eastern Harz region.

In my imagination, I live a great deal out in the countryside, i.e. in the meadows in the woods near Friedrichsbrunn ... I lie on my back in the grass then, feel the light breeze and see the clouds move over the blue sky, while I hear the noises from the wood ... The Central Mountain range is the countryside that belongs to me – the Harz, the Thuringian Forest, the Weser Mountains – or perhaps it is the countryside that has made me what I am. (Letter from Tegel, February 12, 1944)

above:
The garden of the holiday home in Friedrichsbrunn.

center:
With decorated peashooters, the children make their way to the marksmen's procession (from right to left): Karl-Friedrich, Ursula, Dietrich, Walter, Sabine Bonhoeffer, Willi Anschütz, Klaus Bonhoeffer, Hans Anschütz, Christine Bonhoeffer, Lilo Anschütz.

below:
En route from Friedrichsbrunn to Lauer Castle, summer 1914 (from right to left): Ursula, Mrs. Claassen, the governess, Dietrich, Klaus, Christine, Sabine.

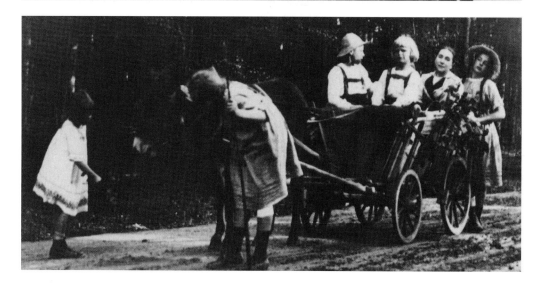

The outbreak of war – the family moves to the Grunewald district

Dietrich Bonhoeffer was eight and a half years old when the First World War broke out. Karl Bonhoeffer has recorded in his memoirs his impressions of those days: "One particularly impressive recollection from that turbulent time is the evening of the day when the English declared war. We were on Unter den Linden with the three boys. On the previous days, the crowds on the streets and in front of the castle and the government offices had felt an increased need to talk to one another. But now, this had given way to a gloomy silence which was quite exceptionally oppressive."

From 1916 onward, the parents were increasingly concerned about finding enough food for their eight growing children. The shortages of milk, fat, and eggs made them decide to keep goats and hens. This was also one reason why the family moved in the spring of 1916 to a house with a garden in Wangenheimstraße 14 in the Grünewald district in Berlin, not far from Halensee railway station.

Fritz Mauthner, the philosopher, and Max Planck, who won the Nobel Prize for physics in 1918, lived here. In the neighboring Kunz-Buntschuh-Straße lived the historian Hans Delbrück, whose "Wednesday circle" included Adolf von Harnack, Friedrich Meinecke, and Ernst Troeltsch. The sons and daughters of these families got to know one another; later, they married each other. And one day they would find themselves side by side in the struggle against Hitler.

above:
The Bonhoeffer family's house,
Wangenheimstraße 14.

left:
Dietrich Bonhoeffer aged 11,
1917.

A middle-class life

The family played music every Saturday evening in the Wangenheimstraße.

All the family came together. We had supper at half-past seven and then we went into the drawing room. Usually, the boys began with a trio: Karl-Friedrich played the piano, Walter the violin, and Klaus the cello. Then "Hörnchen" accompanied my mother as she sang. Each one who had had teaching that week had to present something that evening. Sabine learned the violin, and the two big sisters sang duets as well as Lieder by Schubert, Brahms, and Beethoven. Dietrich was far better at the piano than Karl-Friedrich. (Susanne Dress)

For a period, both Dietrich and his parents thought that he might devote himself to music full-time.

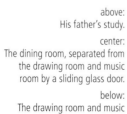

above:
His father's study.

center:
The dining room, separated from the drawing room and music room by a sliding glass door.

below:
The drawing room and music room. Above the piano (left) is a painting of Dietrich's great-grandmother, Pauline von Hase. On the opposite wall, in the oval frame, is the "lovely Miss Bonhöffer" (18th century). Behind the curtained door is the entrance to the smoking room.

The death of his brother

Dietrich's older brother Walter, wounded by mortar fire, died on April 28, 1918, in a field hospital on the Western front. Three hours before his death, he wrote a letter to his parents:

Dear Father and Mother,

I had my second operation today. It was much less agreeable, because deeper splinters were removed. After that, I had to have two injections of camphor – not both at once, of course – but I hope that this means the whole business is over. My technique for thinking "past" the pains has to be used here too. But there are more interesting things in the world than my injury. The battle of Kemmelberg with its potential consequences, and the news we heard today that Ypres is occupied, give us a great deal of hope. I dare not even think of my poor regiment. They had a hard time these last days. I wonder how the other officer cadets are getting on? Now that I am so far away from you, I am thinking of you, dear parents, full of longing, minute by minute throughout the long days and nights.

Your Walter.

When he was confirmed, Dietrich was given Walter's Bible, which he always kept by him.

To our dear Son Walter
on his confirmation day
from his mother.

The letter kills, but
the Spirit makes alive!
(2. Cor 9:6)
So love is
the fulfillment of the law.
(Rom 13:10)

Berlin, March 17, 1914

above:
Dietrich's second oldest brother, Walter.

left:
The dedication by Paula Bonhoeffer in the Bible Walter received when he was confirmed.

The end of the War, the Revolution, and turbulent times

Dietrich, not yet thirteen years old, did not directly experience the struggles between government troops and the Spartakists to get control of the Halensee railway station, near his home: what he experienced was refracted through his parents, as we see from a letter he sent:

Dear grandmother,

Mama is really fine again, despite these disturbances. For a while, she lived with the Schöne family on the other side of the street, and since then she has been much better. You will have read in the newspaper about the attack on the Halensee station. But it wasn't all that dangerous. We could hear everything very clearly, because it happened in the night-time. It all lasted for about an hour, then the rogues were driven off. They tried again at 6 this morning, but all they got this time too was a bleeding head ...

Dietrich attended the Grunewald Grammar School. When the German foreign minister Walther Rathenau was murdered by right-wing irregulars on June 24, 1922, Bonhoeffer sat in his classroom and heard the shots from the Königsallee while the teacher was speaking.

above:
Letter to his grandmother, January 11, 1919 (excerpt).

center:
Intermediary school and high school in Berlin-Grunewald (from 1921 "Grunewald High School," later "Walter Rathenau School"), ca. 1913.

below:
Class O II in the Grunewald High School. From left to right: Elisabeth Caspari, Felix Prentzel, Ursula Andreae (niece of Walter Rathenau), Ellen-Marion Winter (later Countess Peter Yorck), Maria Weigert, teacher Willibald Heininger, Hans-Robert Pfeil, Georg Seligsohn, Dietrich Bonhoeffer, Erdmann Niekisch von Rosenegk, Kurt Mähne, Herbert Mankiewitz (1920/21).

above:
Bonhoeffer in the garden at
Friedrichsbrunn, 1922.

right:
Dietrich Bonhoeffer's copy of
Eduard Meyer's *Origins and
Beginnings of Christianity*.

below:
Bonhoeffer's high school
graduation diploma.

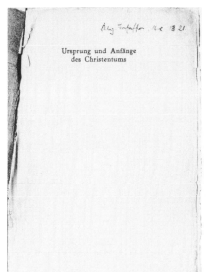

Decision to study theology and high-school graduation

In 1921, Bonhoeffer bought the first two volumes of Eduard Meyer's *Origin and Beginnings
of Christianity*. Although he was still at school, he
added the word "theol." to his name. Despite the
Christian basis provided by his parents' house,
his path to the study of theology began in a sec-
ular environment. First, in youthful decisiveness,
he realized that he was called to do "something"
special; then he became curious about theology
as a science. Unlike theologians who come from
homes conversant with church and theology,
and must first discover that there exists something called a "world," Bonhoeffer left home (so
to speak) in order to discover that there existed
something called the "church."

For his high-school graduation, under his teacher
Walther Kranz, Dietrich chose to write an essay on the subject of "Catullus and Horace as
lyric poets." He concludes with all the pathos
of a sixteen-year-old: "Reflections have never
conquered the world – but feelings have done
so. Even the greatest ideas must pass away, but
feelings remain for ever." His teacher criticized
this remark: "Feelings are insubstantial things. It
is art that remains for ever. And there are also
eternal truths."

Studies
(1923–27)

His siblings/first weddings

In 1923, aged 17, Dietrich went to Tübingen to begin the study of Protestant theology.

In the same year, his elder brother Karl-Friedrich became assistant at the Kaiser Wilhelm Institute for Physical Chemistry. Later he succeeded in demonstrating the existence of the two kinds of hydrogen atoms which were required by quantum theory, and in separating them.

1923 was also the year in which Klaus Bonhoeffer completed his legal studies by taking his doctorate, and Dietrich's sister Ursula married Rüdiger Schleicher, a junior lawyer in the German Transport Ministry and the son of a doctor from Stuttgart.

In 1925, Christine Bonhoeffer married Hans von Dohnanyi, who had been assistant at the Institute for Foreign Politics in Hamburg from 1923.

One year later, Dietrich's twin sister Sabine married Gerhard Leibholz, who became professor of Public Law in Greifswald in 1929.

above left:
Karl-Friedrich Bonhoeffer
(photographed in 1922).

above right:
Rüdiger and Ursula Schleicher
(ca. 1923).

below left:
Christine Bonhoeffer and Hans von Dohnanyi as an engaged couple (1922/23).

below right:
Gerhard and Sabine Leibholz
(ca. 1926).

Tübingen

His father and his elder brothers had already studied in Tübingen. For a time, Dietrich lived there in the house of his grandmother, Julie Bonhoeffer (Neckarhalde 38). Like his father, he joined the student association "Hedgehog" in Tübingen, but he left it in 1935 when it introduced the "Aryan paragraph."

He was especially interested in the famous New Testament scholar Adolf Schlatter (1852–1938). While imprisoned in Tegel in 1943, Bonhoeffer was to recall Schlatter's affirmation that the obligations incumbent on a Christian citizen included bearing with tranquility a period of detention before trial.

Bonhoeffer studied in Tübingen in a time of political unrest and economic inflation. When the military state of emergency was declared in September 1923, in order to preempt both the right-wing preparations for a coup d'état and the threat of left-wing uprisings, Dietrich and other students in Tübingen joined the "Black State Militia" and spent two weeks on military exercises with the riflemen in Ulm. "The State Militia companies make a good impression in general, although almost all of them are extreme reactionaries …"

above:
Gathering of the "Novices" in the "Hedgehog" association, 1923. Wilhelm Dreier is sitting in the front row; to Bonhoeffer's left is Robert Held; to his right is Theodor Pfizer; above him to the right is Arnulf Klett.

below:
The Wilhelmsburg barracks in Ulm.

Adolf Schlatter, ca. 1920.

Rome, 1924

Their parents paid for Dietrich and Klaus to go on a study trip to Rome, and the brothers crossed the Brenner Pass on April 4, 1924. The entries in Dietrich's diary reflect how he experienced the "Eternal city" with its innumerable witnesses to past history and art, and how much he was impressed by the profound piety which linked faith and daily living, doctrine and life:

Classical antiquity is not dead at all ... I was spellbound all the time by the view from the arch of Severus to the Palatine. As I went home, I thought continually: Great Pan is not dead!

When I saw the Laocoon for the first time, a tremor ran right through me. It is unbelievable. Years later, in Tegel, Bonhoeffer recalled this: *When you see the Laocoon again, have a good look and see whether he may be the model for later images of Christ (January 25, 1944).*

Palm Sunday ... the first day on which I understood something real about Catholicism. It has nothing to do with things like Romanticism. No, I think I am beginning to understand the concept of "church."

In Sicily, Klaus and Dietrich were tempted to see Africa with their own eyes. They spent ten days in Tripoli and the Libyan desert. Complications arose, and the two brothers were deported as "unwelcome guests." The diary is silent about the African adventure.

above left:
In Rome,
May 1924.

above right:
Laocoon.

center:
Rome, St Paul's Outside the
Walls. A postcard from Rome
which Bonhoeffer kept.

below:
In the Libyan desert (photograph
taken by D. Bonhoeffer).

above:
Dietrich Bonhoeffer's student
identity card in Berlin.

center:
Adolf von Harnack
(ca. 1920).

below left and right:
"Fifteen Questions" and
"Sixteen Answers" – excerpts
from the debate between Adolf
von Harnack and Karl Barth.

Berlin, 1924/25

The theological faculty at the university, which was a little more than 100 years old at that date, had already made its influence felt in the world. Friedrich Schleiermacher, one of its founders, had been as important in his own time as was Adolf von Harnack, the oldest professor during Bonhoeffer's student days. Although he retired at the age of 70 in 1924, Harnack continued to hold seminars on church history for a select circle. Bonhoeffer attended this special seminar for at least three semesters, and it was here that he gained his first academic plaudits.

In the fall of 1924, Bonhoeffer discovered Karl Barth, in whose collection of essays, published in 1924, he read the following words: God "does not want to be outside this world, posited as it were alongside some worldly existence … His wish is not to provide the basis for a history of religion, but to be … the Lord of our life."

No later than the winter semester of 1924/25, Bonhoeffer was drawn into the controversy which had set people talking all over Germany: in 1923, Adolf von Harnack had published his "Fifteen questions to those theologians who despise academic theology" in the "Christian World." Karl Barth replied with "Sixteen answers" in the following issue.

One year before his death, Adolf von Harnack wrote to Dietrich Bonhoeffer, painting for him a picture of that "intellectual and spiritual existence" which he believed was "threatened by contempt for academic theology and by unacademic theologians": "I am certain that you, dear Mr. Bonhoeffer, will always take this to heart …"

Fünfzehn Fragen an die Verächter der wissenschaftlichen Theologie unter den Theologen

(1) Ist die Religion der Bibel, bzw. sind die Offenbarungen in der Bibel etwas so Einstimmiges, daß man in Hinsicht auf Glauben, Anbetung und Leben einfach von der „Bibel" sprechen darf? Wenn sie es aber nicht sind, darf man die Feststellung des Inhalts des Evangeliums allein der subjektiven „Erfahrung" bzw. dem „Erlebnis" des Einzelnen überlassen, oder sind hier nicht geschichtliches Wissen und kritisches Nachdenken nötig?

. . .

(13) Wenn es gewiß ist, daß alles Unbewußte, Empfindungsmäßige, Numinose, Faszinöse usw. so lange untermenschlich bleibt, als es nicht von der Vernunft ergriffen, begriffen, gereinigt und in seiner berechtigten Eigenart geschützt wird, wie darf man diese Vernunft schelten, ja ausmerzen wollen? Und was hat man zu gewärtigen, wenn dieses herostratische Werk vollbracht ist? Erhebt sich nicht schon jetzt der gnostische Okkultismus auf den Trümmern?

(14) Wenn die Person Jesu Christi im Mittelpunkt des Evangeliums steht, wie läßt sich die Grundlage für eine zuverlässige und gemeinschaftliche Erkenntnis dieser Person anders gewinnen als durch kritisch-geschichtliches Studium, damit man nicht einen erträumten Christus für den wirklichen eintausche? Wer anders aber vermag dieses Studium zu leisten als die wissenschaftliche Theologie?

(15) Gibt es — Trägheit, Kurzsichtigkeit und zahlreiche Krankheiten zugestanden — noch eine andere Theologie als jene, die in fester Verbindung und Blutsverwandtschaft steht mit der Wissenschaft überhaupt? Und wenn es eine solche etwa gibt, welche Überzeugungskraft und welcher Wert kommt ihr zu?

Berlin-Grunewald   Adolf v Harnack

Sechzehn Antworten an Herrn Professor von Harnack
Vgl. Nr. 1.2

(Zum Titel) Wer einen Einwand erhebt gegen die Form protestantisch-wissenschaftlicher Theologie, die sich seit den Tagen des Pietismus und der Aufklärung und im Besondern in den letzten fünfzig Jahren deutscher Vergangenheit als maßgebend herausgebildet hat, braucht darum noch kein „Verächter" der „wissenschaftlichen Theologie" zu sein. Der Einwand lautet dahin, diese Theologie möchte sich mehr als gut ist von ihrem (zuletzt durch die Reformation deutlich gestellten) Thema entfernt haben.

. . .

(15) Wenn die Theologie wieder den Mut zur Sachlichkeit bekäme, den Mut Zeuge des Wortes von der Offenbarung, vom Gericht und von der Liebe Gottes zu werden, so könnte es ja auch so sein, daß „die Wissenschaft überhaupt" nach „fester Verbindung und Blutsverwandtschaft" mit der Theologie ausschauen müßte, statt umgekehrt; denn es stünde vielleicht auch um die Juristen, Mediziner und Philosophen besser, wenn sie wüßten, was die Theologen — wissen sollten. Oder sollte die heutige zufällige opinio communis der Andern wirklich die Instanz sein, von der wir unserm Tun „Überzeugungskraft" und „Wert" zusprechen lassen müßten?

Göttingen   Karl Barth

Work on his dissertation

Bonhoeffer bought Reinhold Seeberg's five volumes on the history of dogma at an early date. Seeberg was professor of systematic theology – Bonhoeffer's favorite subject – in Berlin, and he decided to write his doctorate under him, not under Harnack or Karl Holl (whom he greatly respected).

Alongside his studies and the work on his dissertation, Bonhoeffer had his first experience of work in a parish. He held a "children's sermon," usually prepared beforehand in writing, each Sunday in the Grunewald church.

He had time for leisure activities too: "Dietrich had proposed that we should celebrate the first fine days of spring in April with a long hike across the moors. We all enjoyed ourselves tremendously. We stopped where we liked, and each afternoon we made inquiries about where the nearest village was, then two of us were sent ahead to get a sleeping place ready – never in youth hostels, always in an inn" (Susanne Dress).

In the interval since my last letter and this one, Seeberg returned to Berlin. Since I had already left a message for him, he telephoned me, and since he was staying in Berlin only for one day, he asked me to accompany him to the railway station at 7 in the morning. I had pondered the matter in this way: there is no real point in going to Holl or Harnack to do my work, since I will not meet any opposition at all if I write a dogmatic-historical dissertation under Seeberg. This makes it relatively unimportant to which professor I go with that kind of dissertation, since I believe that Seeberg's attitude is generally positive. So I stuck with Seeberg, and I now suggested to him a subject that is half historical and half systematic, and which he completely accepted. It is connected with the theme of the religious community – I told you one evening some time ago that that would interest me. It requires a great deal of historical research, but that won't do me any harm at all. Anyway, Seeberg too seems greatly interested in the work, and he said that he had been waiting for a long time for a student who would work in this field, and that it was wonderful that I had hit upon this idea all by myself. Then, without explicitly mentioning his conversation with you, dear Papa, he apparently referred to what you had said, and assured me that it would all go very well – he had seen this from the quality of the work I did for him before! When I laughed a little at these words, he repeated them! Well, I have reached a firm agreement with him about this matter, and I believe that this was absolutely the right thing to do.

From a letter to his parents, September 21, 1925.

Reinhold Seeberg

Walking over the moors, April 1927: from the left, Walter and Ilse Dress, Dietrich and Susanne Bonhoeffer, Grete von Dohnanyi (later the wife of Karl-Friedrich Bonhoeffer).

Doctorate

On December 17, 1927, in the old Hall of the university of Berlin, Bonhoeffer publicly defended the theses of his dissertation. The first phase of his academic career concluded with the degree of Licentiate in theology (lic. theol.).

At Christmas 1927, all the family came together in the Wangenheimstraße. Within the space of one year, Karl-Friedrich had written his Habilitation dissertation (enabling him to become a professor); Klaus had completed his studies and was now a junior lawyer; and Dietrich had finished his doctoral work. For the first time since Walter's death, Karl Bonhoeffer made an entry in his diary for New Year's Eve: "Christmas this year, when we once again have all our beloved children here with us, prompts me to open this old book anew ... In the spring, we had a great fancy-dress ball here in the house ... This evening, the Schleichers and Dohnanyis are with us, Karl-Friedrich, Claus, and Dietrich. He will probably be in Barcelona next year."

When the family celebrated Christmas in 1930, Dietrich Bonhoeffer was in the USA. He was sent the family photograph as a present.

THEOLOGISCHE THESEN

WELCHE MIT GENEHMIGUNG
DES
HERRN DEKANS DER HOCHWÜRDIGEN THEOLOGISCHEN FAKULTÄT
AN DER
Friedrich-Wilhelms-Universität
zu Berlin
ZUR
ERWERBUNG DES GRADES EINES LIZENTIATEN DER THEOLOGIE
AM 17. DEZEMBER 1927 12 UHR MITTAGS
IN DER ALTEN AULA
ÖFFENTLICH VERTEIDIGEN WIRD
DIETRICH BONHOEFFER

OPPONENTEN:
HERR CAND. THEOL. ROBERT STUPPERICH
HERR LIC. THEOL. WALTER DRESS
HERR VIKAR HELMUTH ROESSLER

BERLIN
FUCHSDRUCKEREI EMIL EBERING, MITTELSTRASSE 19

SANCTORUM COMMUNIO

EINE DOGMATISCHE UNTERSUCHUNG
ZUR SOZIOLOGIE DER KIRCHE

VON
Lic. DIETRICH BONHOEFFER

DIE DRUCKLEGUNG ERFOLGTE
MIT UNTERSTÜTZUNG DER NOTGEMEINSCHAFT
DER DEUTSCHEN WISSENSCHAFT

TROWITZSCH & SOHN · BERLIN UND FRANKFURT/ODER
1930

above:
Doctoral dissertation "Sanctorum Communio." First page of the typewritten manuscript, with endorsements by Professors Arthur Titius and Reinhold Seeberg.

center left:
Announcement of the public defense of the dissertation theses.

center right:
First edition of the doctoral dissertation, 1930.

below:
Christmas 1927.

Barcelona–Berlin–New York
(1928–32)

Bonhoeffer took his first theological examination at the Consistory of the Brandenburg district in January 1928 and received the mark "very good." At the suggestion of Superintendent Max Diestel, who was his superior, he went in February to work for a year as vicar in the Protestant parish for foreigners in Barcelona.

Superintendent Max Diestel, ca. 1930.

This parish numbered about 300; there were 6,000 persons in the German colony at that time. "They have the same positive attitude to the church as to sport or to the German National Party, but they are less active." Bonhoeffer joined the "German Club," the German tennis and song society, and he put his skills in music and in chess to good use. "There is only one thing I can't do – play skat. But I really need to play it well here; so perhaps I will learn this too."

Bonhoeffer was particularly involved in children's worship and in youth work. He gave religious instruction at the German school in Barcelona. The last entry in his Spanish diary reads: "My theology is beginning to turn humanistic; what does this mean? I wonder if Barth was ever in foreign parts?"

He also visited Cordoba, Seville, Granada, and Madrid, and described his experiences at a bullfight in the arena: "Altogether, there is a mighty portion of passion raging in the people here, and one is drawn into it oneself. Here is the remnant of an unrestricted, passionate life."

above:
A parish celebration in Barcelona, 1928.

below:
Dietrich Bonhoeffer with participants in the children's services in Barcelona, 1928.

above:
A parish celebration in
Barcelona, 1928.

below left:
"Greetings from the matador":
A signed postcard sent by
Dietrich Bonhoeffer from
Barcelona to his brother-in-law,
Rüdiger Schleicher.

below right:
The German school in Barcelona

Berlin, 1929–1930

Back in Germany, the foreign minister, Gustav Stresemann, died on October 3, 1929. It was not by chance that in the same year Joseph Goebbels, the "regional commander" of Berlin, was appointed head of Nazi propaganda in Germany. At this period, only 2.9 per cent of voters supported the party. At the end of March 1930, Heinrich Brüning became chancellor for the first time, and the period of "emergency ordinances" began. This was the last attempt to save the Weimar republic.

After his first experience of pastoral work in church and society in Barcelona, Bonhoeffer returned with a new passion to his theological work and began his Habilitation dissertation. He may have been referring later on to this phase of his life when he wrote self-critically: "I plunged into my work … My ambition – something many people have observed in me – made my life difficult."

Adolf von Harnack died on June 10, 1930. In the name of his former students, Dietrich Bonhoeffer held an address: "I believe that he would approve if I conclude with a sentence that he himself held very dear. A year ago, on a summer excursion, this was the last word he spoke to his old seminar: *Non potest non laetari, qui sperat in Dominum* [One who hopes in the Lord cannot do anything else than rejoice]."

above left:
Adolf von Harnack in the last year of his life.

above right:
Printed program for the memorial service in honor of Adolf von Harnack, June 15, 1930.

below:
Manuscript of the first lecture, July 31, 1930.

above:
Second theological examination certificate.

below :
Notification of the successful Habilitation.

On July 8, Bonhoeffer took his second theological examination. On July 12, his Habilitation was approved, and he held his first lecture on July 31 on "The question of the human person in contemporary philosophy and theology." His Habilitation dissertation, "Act and Being," was published in 1931.

Dietrich Bonhoeffer's Habilitation dissertation.

Theologische Jakultät
der
Wilhelms-Univerſität

Tgb. Nr. 730.

Berlin C 2, den ......1. Auguſt...... 1930.
227

UI 7649 30

Preuß. Ministerium f. Wissenschaft,
Kunst u. Volksbildung
Eing.: 1. AUG. 1930

Dem Herrn Minister beehre ich mich zu berichten, dass sich Herr Lic. B o n h o e f f e r am 12. Juli 1930 in der theologischen Fakultät für systematische Theologie habilitiert hat.

Ich beehre mich beizufügen:

1.) einen Lebenslauf,

2.) einen Personalbogen,

3.) ein Licentiatendiplom,

4.) das Schriftenverzeichnis.

Die Licentiatendissertation erscheint in etwa 8 Tagen in umgearbeiteter Form im Druck und wird dann sogleich eingeliefert.

Die Habilitationsschrift,die noch nicht gedruck ist, wird nachgereicht werden.

Sie behandelt das Thema:

"Akt und Sein" Transzendentalphilosophie und Ontologie in der systematischen Theologie.

D e r   D e k a n

Minister für Wissenschaft,
und Volksbildung
lin W 8.
en Linden 4.

Studies in New York, 1930

On September 5, 1930, Bonhoeffer departed for studies in New York. He had received a grant for this purpose, after achieving brilliant results in the academic and the ecclesiastical spheres at the beginning of his career. He had never been so free before; and he was never again to experience this freedom, the sense of having done all that was required, the sense that every door stood open.

Bonhoeffer studied at Union Theological Seminary, which was then at the height of its fame. It already had ecumenical ambitions and attracted many European guests. It was headed by Henry Sloane Coffin, a "church statesman" and a great preacher at the central Presbyterian Church on Madison Avenue. Reinhold Niebuhr was appointed professor of "Applied Christianity" in 1928. H.E. Ward gave a course on "Ethical Interpretations" and got his students to investigate systems of insurance for the unemployed and the results of the bank crash. Bonhoeffer learned that 350,000 investors had lost their small savings; the sums involved went up to 400 dollars. He noted: "The stronger banks are the principal masters of America."

D. Bonhoeffer with the children of the Ern family, whom he met on board ship.

above:
D. Bonhoeffer (center) waving to his parents as the ship leaves Bremerhaven.

below:
Union Theological Seminary, 1931. President H. S. Coffin, Prof. Swift, Prof. R. Niebuhr, Prof. H. E. Ward
(from right to left).

above:
In the garden of Union
Theological Seminary,
summer 1930.

New York, photographs
taken by D. Bonhoeffer:

center left:
Union Theological Seminary;
tower of Riverside Church in
the background;

center right:
The "Union"; in the fore-
ground, the President's
Suite;

below left:
Tower of Riverside Church
with Grant's Memorial;

below right:
George Washington Bridge.

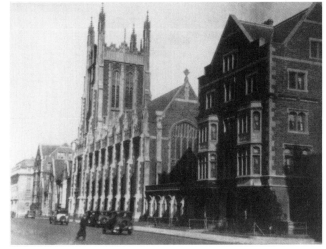

"The seminary is a place where each one may speak freely with all the others ...," yet Bonhoeffer could not initially find what he was accustomed to: "There is no theology here." Nevertheless, toward the end of his study period, he wrote: "The impression I have received from today's representatives of the social gospel will leave a decisive imprint on me for a long time."

Thanks to his student friend Frank Fisher (nr. 9 in the group photo), Bonhoeffer had intensive contacts with the reality of life in Harlem: "For more than six months, I went almost every Sunday afternoon at two-thirty to one of the big Negro Baptist churches in Harlem ... I have heard the gospel preached in the Negro churches." He helped in the Sunday school in the Abyssinian Baptist Church at 128 West 138th Street.

The house of Paul and Marion Lehmann became a place where Bonhoeffer encountered faithful friendship. In 1939, Paul Lehmann was to do everything in his power to keep Dietrich in the country and to save him.

Union Theological Seminary: D. Bonhoeffer, Klemm, Marion und Paul Lehmann, Erwin Sutz, 1931.

above:
Union Theological Seminary New York, 1930/31. 1. Prof. Fleming, 2. Prof. Scott, 3. Prof. Ward, 4. Prof. Niebuhr, 5. President Coffin, 6. Prof. Baillie, 7. Prof. Bewer, 8. Prof. Moffat, 9. Frank Fisher, 10. Paul Lehmann, 11. Erwin Sutz, 12. Dietrich Bonhoeffer.

below:
A shopfront church in Harlem.

above left:
Christmas 1930, with Erwin Sutz
(a Swiss) in Havana, Cuba.

above right:
With Jean Lasserre (left) in
Mexico, 1931.

center:
Repairing the car which the Ern
family had lent them for this trip.

below:
Paul Lehmann, Dietrich Bonhoeffer, a policeman, Erwin Sutz,
near Cleveland, Ohio.

Cuba and Mexico

Bonhoeffer spent Christmas 1930 in Cuba with
Erwin Sutz. He painted a gloomy picture in his
address to the members of the German colony
in the Christmas service: he found it "especially
strange to celebrate Christmas in this year, when
throngs of unemployed people stand before our
eyes." Who could then "enter the promised land
without inhibitions, and without being aware of
what is going on? Perhaps the children can man-
age this." Bonhoeffer had chosen an unusual
text, the story of Moses on Mount Nebo, who
must die on the threshold to the land for which
he has yearned (Deut 32:48–52).

At the end of his year of study in America, Bonhoeffer went with Jean Lasserre to Mexico. Paul
Lehmann and Erwin Sutz accompanied them as
far as Chicago. In his conversations with Lasserre,
Bonhoeffer found a new access to the Sermon on
the Mount. Was this the first inspiration for his
later book on discipleship? Lasserre was present
at Bonhoeffer's "peace speech" in Fanö. In the
letters from Tegel, he speaks of the deep impression that this French pastor had made on him.

Developments
(1931–32)

Return to Germany, 1931

Bonhoeffer returned from America to a country where political, social, and economic conditions were heading toward chaos. After the Müller government had fallen in March 1930, the Central Party politician Heinrich Brüning had attempted by means of emergency ordinances to combat the consequences of the financial crisis. He lowered wages and salaries, prices, government expenditure, and aid to the unemployed, while at the same time raising taxes. The Nazis exploited this policy of the "hunger Chancellor" in their demagogy against "the system." They became a mass movement that increasingly determined the course of German politics.

Nevertheless, things looked well for Bonhoeffer when he began to teach as a "Privatdozent" at the Friedrich-Wilhelm University in summer of 1931. At that date, the theological faculty had ca. 1,000 students; the lecture and seminar rooms were filled to capacity.

In July, Bonhoeffer met Karl Barth in Bonn: "I am even more impressed by the way he discusses things than by his writings and lectures. When he speaks, he is 100 per cent present. I have never seen anything like that before." From now on, through varying phases of intimacy and distance, the two theologians were to join forces in the church-political struggle.

above:
The bank collapse in 1931. Thousands of Berliners waited in line to withdraw their money.

center:
The Friedrich-Wilhelm University in Berlin.

below:
Karl Barth, ca. 1930.

... I plunged into my work in a very un-Christian and un-humble manner. A crazy ambition – something many people have observed in me – made my life difficult and led my fellow human beings to withdraw their love and trust from me. That was terrible.

Then something else arrived, that has kept on transforming my life until now, and turned it upside-down: for the first time, I came to the Bible. And that too is a dreadful thing to say. I had often preached, I had already seen a great deal of the church, and I had spoken and written about it – but I had not yet become a Christian. I was still the lord of my own life, completely wild and untamed. I know that I made the cause of Christ a matter of my own advantage, something promoting my own mad vanity, at that time, and I ask God that this may never happen again. And I had never prayed – or only very little. Despite my abandoned state, I was well content with myself. The Bible freed me from this – and especially the Sermon on the Mount.

Since then, everything is different. Not only I myself have felt this clearly – others around me have sensed it too. That was a tremendous liberation. It became clear to me at that time that the life of a servant of Jesus Christ must belong to the church, and step by step it became clearer how far the consequences of this truth must reach ... Only a short time before this, I had fought passionately ... against Christian pacifism. Now, it seemed to me the most obvious thing in the world.

Dietrich Bonhoeffer to Elisabeth Zinn, 1936.

Lecturing work, 1931–1932

At some point early on in his career as lecturer, Bonhoeffer was "transformed from a theologian into a Christian" (E. Bethge). He himself scarcely ever spoke of this directly; the only allusion is in a self-critical letter to Elisabeth Zinn (January, 1936; see left), and here the perspective is altogether too sharp.

In the summer semester of 1932, Bonhoeffer offered exercises in systematic theology and lectures on ecclesiology. His seminar, evenings which were open to all the students, and excursions led to the formation of a "Bonhoeffer circle" among the students. Later, a number of them would work closely with him in the "church struggle"; but in 1932, all they did was to bring potatoes, flour, and vegetables in a wheelbarrow to the Stettin railway station and then spend the weekend together on the moors.

In the winter semester of 1932/33, Bonhoeffer lectured on "Creation and sin: A theological exposition of Gen 1-3." The reaction was so great that his students persuaded him to have his manuscript printed.

A weekend course in Prebelow. D. Bonhoeffer with his Berlin students, 1932.

DIETRICH BONHOEFFER

Schöpfung und Fall

Theologische Auslegung von Genesis 1—3

1933

Chr. Kaiser Verlag / München

Title page of the publication of his lectures in book form.

The annual assembly of the World Alliance for Promoting International Firiendship through the Churches was held in Cambridge from September 1 to 5, 1931. Superintendent Max Diestel proposed Bonhoeffer as one of the delegation of young German Christians.

On the morning of the opening day, an article in the *Hamburger Nachrichten* caused a furor. It was entitled: "The Protestant Church and Understanding between the Peoples," and the right-wing press was exultant. Two professors of theology, Paul Althaus (Erlangen) and Emanuel Hirsch (Göttingen) declared, in view of the "dictated peace of Versailles": "In this situation, we believe that the only possible 'understanding' between us Germans and the nations who won the victory in the World War is to testify to them that no 'understanding' can come about as long as they continue their war against us."

In Cambridge, Bonhoeffer was elected as one of the three honorary youth secretaries. This made him a member of the Management Committee and the Council. Six months after the conference, he summed the situation up as follows: "The results of the Cambridge conference in Germany are few, because nationalistic professors of theology fight against the work of the World Alliance."

As youth secretary of the World Alliance, Bonhoeffer worked with the "German Intermediary Center for Ecumenical Youth Work" in Berlin. On the national level, the difficulties increased: the World Alliance was accused of "internationalism" and "pacifist tendencies." In 1932 and 1933, the annual assemblies of the World Alliance, which had been planned for Germany, had to be canceled.

The declaration "Protestant Church and Understanding between the Peoples."

Evangelische Kirche und Völkerverständigung

Eine Erklärung *)

Das deutsche Volk ist in einem von ihm nicht gewollten, ihm aufgezwungenen Kriege niedergerungen und durch Friedensdiktat des Anteils an der Verwaltung von Raum und Gütern der Erde beraubt worden, den es braucht, um auch nur atmen und leben zu können. Es wird überdies durch Kriegskontributionen unter dem lügnerischen Namen der Wiedergutmachung bis zum Weißbluten ausgesogen. Alles das unter offenem Bruche der Zusagen, die ihm bei der Waffenniederlegung gemacht worden sind, und unter abermals offenem Bruch der im Friedensvertrage von jenen Nationen feierlich übernommenen Verpflichtung auf Abrüstung. Deutschlands Feinde aus dem Weltkriege führen also unter dem Deckmantel des Friedens den Krieg wider das deutsche Volk weiter und vergiften durch die darin liegende Unwahrheit die politische Weltlage so, daß Aufrichtigkeit und Vertrauen unmöglich werden. Das Ende dieses nun schon zwölf Jahre währenden neuen furchtbaren Krieges mitten im Frieden kann, wenn er auch nur kurze Zeit fortgesetzt wird, allein der Untergang unseres Volkes sein.

In dieser Lage gibt es nach unserem Urteil zwischen uns Deutschen und den im Weltkriege siegreichen Nationen keine andere Verständigung als ihnen zu bezeugen, daß während ihres fortgesetzten Krieges wider uns eine Verständigung nicht möglich ist. Es gibt in unserer Lage vorerst keine andere aufrichtige Pflege der Gemeinschaft, als daß man ihren trügerischen Schein zerstört und das Verhältnis der andern Nationen zu uns bei seinem richtigen Namen nennt. Wer diese wirkliche Lage, wer den Bruch der Gemeinschaft, den sie bedeutet, mit Worten oder durch sein Verhalten, verhüllt, der wird schuldig an allen denen innerhalb der anderen Völker, die das Rechte wollen: er tut nicht das Seine dazu, daß sie die Wirklichkeit des Schicksals sehen lernen, das ihre Völker dem deutschen Volke bereiten. Er hilft die Verlogenheit der internationalen Lage erhalten und steigern.

Der hier vertretene Grundsatz hindert nicht ein Zusammenkommen und Zusammenarbeiten mit einzelnen Gliedern der unser Leben bedrohenden Nation an besonderen, begrenzten und dringlichen Aufgaben; die Schicksalsverflochtenheit bleibt unentrinnbar auch in dieser furchtbaren Lage. Es bleibt auch dem Einzelnen seine Gewissensfreiheit, ob er über den klaffenden Riß hinweg, unter offenem Vorbehalt und Bekenntnisse eben dieses Risses und Bruches, ein rein privates, persönliches Verhältnis mit Einzelnen aus jenen Nationen pflegen will. Das alles ist bestimmt begrenzt oder privat: indem es sich dessen bewußt ist, gefährdet es die Klarheit und Wahrheit des öffentlichen Gewissens nicht. Aber Worte und Begegnungen können eine Öffentlichkeit und eine Grundsätzlichkeit gewinnen, die ihnen entscheidende Bedeutung für die Gestaltung des allgemeinen Gewissens gibt. Das ist überall dort der Fall, wo Vertreter deutscher Theologie oder deutschen Kirchentums von dem Verhältnis zwischen den Völkern und von der Verständigung verantwortlich reden oder mit Vertretern der Theologie oder des Kirchentums der uns aussaugenden und bedrückenden Nationen sich begegnen. Hier bekommt die Forderung volle Wucht: durch allen künstlichen Schein der Gemeinschaft hindurchzustoßen und rückhaltlos zu bekennen, daß eine christliche und kirchliche Verständigung und Zusammenarbeit in den Fragen der Annäherung der Völker unmöglich ist, solange die Andern eine für unser Volk mörderische Politik gegen uns treiben. Wer da glaubt, der Verständigung heute anders dienen zu können als so, der verleugnet das deutsche Schicksal und verwirrt die Gewissen im Inlande und Auslande, weil er hier der Wahrheit nicht die Ehre gibt.

Professor D. P. Althaus, Erlangen
Professor D. E. Hirsch, Göttingen

From July 20 to 31, 1932, Bonhoeffer took part in the International Youth Peace Conference in Ciernohorské Kúpele in the Carpathians. On July 26, he delivered a lecture on "The theological basis of the World Alliance."

From August 19 to 22, 1932, the Management Committee of the World Alliance met in Geneva. Bonhoeffer was surprised when Wilfried Monod, whom the Germans were accustomed to regard as a hard-line French nationalist, made the same demand in a memorandum that Bonhoeffer had already made in Ciernohorské Kúpele: viz., a presentation of the biblical and systematic foundations of the principles governing the search for Christian unity, the goals of peace, and the path to be followed. After this meeting, the youth conference of the World Alliance was held in Gland on Lake Geneva. Bonhoeffer led the German working party. At the close of the conference, he said: "We are not an organization serving some goal of church activity. Rather, we are one particular form taken by the church itself ... The World Alliance is the terrified, timorous church of Christ which has pricked up its ears and now calls on its Lord to come."

above:
The Management Committee of the World Alliance in Geneva, August 19–22, 1932.
Sitting 4th from left Henriod (Geneva), 6th from left Dickinson (London), Amundsen (Denmark), far right Richter (Berlin). Middle row, 8th from left Siegmund-Schultze (Berlin), 13th from left Maas (Heidelberg). Upper row 4th from left Leiper (USA), Wissing (Holland), Karlström (Sweden), Toureille (France), Bonhoeffer, Craske (England).

right:
Dietrich Bonhoeffer during the conference in Gland.

Participants at the youth conference in Gland. Seated in 2nd row Steele (Geneva), Bonhoeffer, Henriod (Geneva), Burroughs (England), Toureille (France), Craske (England). Two rows above Craske: D. von Oppen.

"Auxiliary service" and social involvement

At the same time as he began lecturing, Bonhoeffer – who was subject to the provisions of the "Church law about the employment of candidates for the parochial ministry in the 'emergency service' of the church" – was commissioned on June 12, 1931 "to carry out the auxiliary service as city vicar in Berlin until further notice."

He was ordained in St Matthew's Church in the Tiergarten district of Berlin on November 15, and was student chaplain at the Technical College in Charlottenburg until 1933. It was difficult to work in this world influenced by technological rationalism, and the posters he put up were torn down.

At the end of 1931, the Consistory instructed him to take over a class preparing for confirmation in the Zion parish in the Prenzlauer Berg district. As he wrote to Erwin Sutz, "This is more or less the craziest district in Berlin, with the most difficult social and political situation." At the beginning of January 1932, Bonhoeffer rented a room from baker Heide in Oderberger Straße 61, north of Alexanderplatz.

Dietrich Bonhoeffer in the fall of 1932.

above:
Instructions from the Consistory of the Brandenburg district, June 12, 1931.

center:
St Matthew's Church, Tiergarten district, Berlin.

below:
Note addressed in Bonhoeffer's handwriting "To the student, who felt compelled to remove this notice for the third time!"

right page:

above:
D. Bonhoeffer with confirmands from Berlin in Friedrichsbrunn, Easter 1932.

below:
Dietrich Bonhoeffer in front of the weekend hut in Biesenthal which his parents gave him for use in his youth work.

To begin with, he let the confirmands run wild. Then he stood against the wall, without saying a word – and then he began to speak very quietly about the black youngsters in Harlem. The confirmands' only option was to listen, and they were soon fascinated. Gradually, Bonhoeffer achieved a close contact to them. Finally, he and his mother saw to it that each of them received a suit for the confirmation. After the service, Bonhoeffer and his cousin Hans Christoph von Hase went to the holiday house of his parents in Friedrichsbrunn with some of the confirmands.

In summer of 1932, Bonhoeffer was involved in the planning and foundation of a "youth room" for unemployed young people. Anneliese Schnurmann, a school friend of his sister Susanne, made money available for social-educational work. He drew on the experiences of Friedrich Siegmund-Schultze and his Social Workers' Fellowship in East Berlin. The "youth room" opened its doors in Charlottenburg in the fall of 1932. After January 30, 1933, communist visitors encountered difficulties on the streets. Bonhoeffer hid them away for a time in a hut in Biesenthal, which his parents had given him for use in his youth work. Then the "youth room" had to be closed down. He had hitherto been concerned for those excluded from the world of work. Now his concern was for others who were stigmatized much more radically – the Jews. Anneliese Schnurmann, who herself was affected by the new conditions, was forced to emigrate.

Oderberger Str. 61.

Decision
(1933)

"On the Führer's responsibility"

At midday on January 30, 1933, President von Hindenburg charged Adolf Hitler to form a government. The first words uttered by Rudiger Schleicher – Dietrich's brother-in-law – that same evening as he entered the room at home were: "This means war!" All the Bonhoeffers, including Dietrich, said the same.

On February 1, Bonhoeffer gave a radio talk on "The Führer and the Individual in the Young Generation" (see center right). The management of the radio program switched him off before he finished his talk, and Bonhoeffer sent an explanatory circular letter to his friends "in order to ward off any misunderstandings."

The complete text of the lecture was published in the "Kreuzzeitung." Under the heading "Service of the State," Bonhoeffer concluded: "In sober realism, [the Führer] must limit himself to his own task. He is at the service of the good order of the state, i.e., of society, and his service can have incomparable value; indeed, it may be indispensable. However, in this service of the other authority, the Führer points to that ultimate authority of which the state and society are merely penultimate authorities. Only a Führer who himself serves both the penultimate and the ultimate authorities will receive loyalty."

This lecture is an attack on the "German Christians," who had been founded in the spring of 1932 by J. Hossenfelder, a pastor in Berlin. They wanted to unite the federal-state churches to form one single national Protestant church. While Bonhoeffer was showing the city to his American friends Paul and Marion Lehmann, who stayed in Berlin at the beginning of April, the national assembly of the German Christians was taking place on April 3 and 4 under slogans such as: "bringing into line," "the Führer principle," "state church," or "racially appropriate."

Human persons – especially young people – will have the need to appoint a Führer to lead them until they feel themselves sufficiently mature, strong, and responsible to fulfill in their own persons the claim that they make of this authority. The Führer must be responsibly aware of this clear limit to his own authority. If he understands his function otherwise than in keeping with the nature of the matter, he will fail to inform clearly those whom he leads about the limitation of his task and about the responsibility which is genuinely incumbent upon this task. Those whom he leads will always want him to embody their idol. But if he lets himself be carried away by the people, and accepts this expectation, the image of the Führer will slip over into the image of the seducer [Verführer].

Excerpt from Bonhoeffer's radio broadcast, February 1, 1933.

above:
Hitler's cabinet,
January 30, 1933.

below:
Circular letter to
Bonhoeffer's friends.

Lic. Bonhoeffer Privatdozent.   Berlin, den 2. II. 33.
Studentenpfarrer an der
Technischen Hochschule.
Grunewald Wangenheimstr. 14.

　　　Um einem etwaigen Mißverstndnis vorzubeugen, das sich bei
demjenigen, der am 1. Februar 5,45 zufllig meinen Rundfunkvortrag
über die „Wandlungen des Führerbegriffs in der jungen Generation"
gehört hat, einstellen könnte, erlaube ich mir mitzuteilen, daß
die Übertragung des Vortrags wegen geringer Zeitüberschreitung
plötzlich an einer völlig ungeeigneten, zu Misdeutungen Anlaß ge-
benden Stelle abgebrochen wurde, sodaß die mir wesentlichsten
wenigen Schlußstze, in denen die theologische Abgrenzung voll-
zogen werden sollte, ganz zum Wegfall kamen und das Gesamtbild
dadurch entstellt erscheinen mußte. Der Vortrag wird nunmehr in ei:
einer Tageszeitung veröffentlicht werden.

　　　　　　　　gez.

　　　　　　　　Bonhoeffer.

National assembly of the German Christians in the former Prussian Upper Chamber in Berlin (April 3, 1933). Pastor Peter holds his lecture on "Church and People." In the president's chair: Pastor Hossenfelder.

The Reichstag fire and the "Reichstag Fire Ordinance"

On February 27, 1933, the Reichstag (German parliament) went up in flames, and the Dutch communist Marinus van der Lubbe was accused of arson. The Ministry of Justice asked Hans von Dohnanyi to take part in the trial as an observer. When van der Lubbe went on a hunger strike, the investigating judge asked Karl Bonhoeffer to write a psychological report.

One day later, on February 28, the President published, at Hitler's demand, the momentous "Ordinance of the Federal President for the Protection of the People and the State." The "Reichstag Fire Ordinance" annulled the personal rights that were guaranteed by the constitution and made possible the construction of the concentration camps. K.D. Bracher has written: "This was the basic 'emergency law' on which the Nazi dictatorship ... seized as its priority." Bonhoeffer's seminar in Finkenwalde was shut down in 1937 on the basis of this ordinance.

To begin with, however, Hitler attended the official ceremony in the Garrison Church in Potsdam on March 21, 1933, which marked the opening of the new parliament. He presented himself as a man who honored tradition and authority. The wide diffusion of a photograph showing him bowing his head before the aged Federal President von Hindenburg no doubt helped him gain a large measure of support in conservative bourgeois circles.

above left:
February 27, 1933:
the Reichstag in flames.
above right:
Marinus van der Lubbe.
center and below:
"Ordinance of the Federal President for the Protection of the People and the State, February 27, 1933."

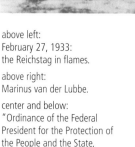

Chancellor Adolf Hitler takes leave of Federal president Hindenburg, March 21, 1933.

above:
An SA man and civilians in front of a Jewish shop.

center left:
Gerhard Leibholz, who took up a full professorship at the university of Göttingen in 1931.

center right:
Franz Hildebrandt.

below:
"The Church Confronted by the Jewish Question": part of the first page of the manuscript.

"The church confronted by the Jewish question"

At 10 a.m. on April 1, 1933, SA and SS troops took up position before Jewish businesses: "German people! Defend yourself! Don't buy from the Jew!" Only one week later, on April 7, 1933, the "Law for the Restoration of the Professional Civil Office System" began the dismantling of the rights of the German Jews: this law led to the dismissal of "non-Aryan" civil servants (and of those whose politics were unacceptable).

The treatment of "non-Aryans" by the Third Reich affected the family directly. Gerhard Leibholz, the husband of Dietrich's twin sister Sabine, and Franz Hildebrandt, Dietrich's closest friend, as well as many other friends of the family and assistants of Dietrich's father, were now ostracized and compelled to emigrate. Many anxious debates on political questions took place in the Wangenheimstraße. Plans for church-political action were also discussed.

The persecution of the Jews in Germany was the main reason why Bonhoeffer joined the political resistance. In "The Church Confronted by the Jewish Question," written in April, 1933, he says:

A state which puts the Christian proclamation at risk, denies its own self. This means that the church has three possibilities of action in relation to the state: first (as we have said), it can ask the state to demonstrate that its actions are legitimate and may properly be undertaken by a state ... Second, we can care for the victims of the state's actions. The church is absolutely bound to help the victims of every social ordering, even where these persons do not belong to the Christian community ... The third possibility means not only binding up the wounds of those crushed by the wheel, but also trying to stop the wheel in its course. That would be directly political behavior on the part of the church.

"On the question of the national bishop"

After Hitler seized power, the German Christians intensified their efforts to achieve a unified national church – an idea which was popular in the federal-state churches. Hitler appointed Ludwig Müller, pastor of the Königsberg military district, as his commissioner for the affairs of the Protestant church. In order to preserve their independence, the federal-state churches elected Pastor D. Friedrich von Bodelschwingh as their national bishop on May 27, 1933. This led the German Christians to agitate all the more strongly against Bodelschwingh and in favor of Müller.

At the University of Berlin, the Student Campaign Association of German Christians undertook a massive propaganda exercise on behalf of Müller. With the student chaplain Bronisch-Holtze, Bonhoeffer intervened in the national chancellery.

On June 22, the church opposition organized a meeting in the New Lecture Room. Emmanuel Hirsch (spokesman of the German Christians) and Professors Deissmann, Sellin, Lütgert, Schumann (spokesmen of the "church center party") and Dietrich Bonhoeffer (spokesman of the "young reformers") spoke.

above left:
Friedrich von Bodelschwingh (center).

above right:
Military district pastor Ludwig Müller (center).

center:
Memorandum from the National Chancellery, June 20, 1933.

The deepest impression on the meeting was made by the words of lecturer Bonhoeffer, when he indicated the possibilities and limits of a battle within the church. This "battle" is permissible only where all involved are aware of the forgiveness of sins and act in the spirit of the words: "Do not judge." In keeping with Rom 14, the weak in faith, who want to erect before the entrance to the church a law like that of the Aryan paragraph, must be borne fraternally by those who are strong in faith. But if the law of the weak were truly to be elevated to the law of the church, this would be a matter that only a Protestant council could decide. Prescinding from the prophetic and reforming possibility that God may reveal himself to an individual, such a council is the authoritative body on all questions that touch the substance of the church, and it would then have to pronounce on the unity or schism of the church. While the church ought to thank God for the hour in which she is called to profess her faith, she must never forget that God's highest gift to his church is peace. It is worth informing the Christian community that it was possible to say this in an assembly filled to overflowing – and indeed that a calm atmosphere prevailed.

From a report in the periodical *Junge Kirche*.

zugesagte freie wahl des kirchenvolkes unmoeglich gemacht da
saemtlich vorhandenes material soeben 19,25 uhr in der reichsleitung
des wahlvorschlages evangelische kirche durch geheime staatspolizei
beschlagnahmt =

reichsleitung mirbachstr 24 +

Jede Glaubensbewegung, die keine Schwärmerei sein will,
muß sich vor dem Wort Gottes verantworten!

DIE DEUTSCHEN CHRISTEN SAGEN: Des Volkes Stimme ist Gottes Stimme
 (Erklärung Müller 14.7.33)
DIE BIBEL SAGT: Wer aus der Wahrheit ist, der höret meine Stimme.
 Da schrieen sie wieder allesamt und sprachen: Nicht
 diesen, sondern Barrabas! — Barrabas aber war ein
 Mörder. (Joh.18,37,40)

DIE DEUTSCHEN CHRISTEN SAGEN: Das Erscheinen Jesu Christi in der Welt-
 geschichte ist in seinem letzten Gehalt ein Aufflammen
 nordischer Art. (Jaeger 13.7.)
DIE BIBEL SAGT: Dies ist das Buch von der Geburt Jesu Christi, der da
 ist ein Sohn Davids, des Sohns Abrahams. (Matth.1,1)

DIE DEUTSCHEN CHRISTEN SAGEN: Ein gottloser Volksgenosse steht uns näher
 als ein volksfremder, auch wenn er das gleiche Lied singt
 oder das gleiche Gebet betet. (Hossenfelder,Hamburg 1.7.)
DIE BIBEL SAGT: Wer Gottes Willen tut, der ist mein Bruder und meine
 Schwester und meine Mutter. (Mark.3,35)

DIE DEUTSCHEN CHRISTEN SAGEN: Nur das Bestehen der Nation ermöglicht das
 Bestehen einer geordneten und dadurch arbeitsfähigen Kir-
 che. (Jaeger, Ev.Dtschld.2.7.)
DIE BIBEL SAGT: Du bist Petrus, und auf diesen Fels will ich bauen meine
 Gemeinde und die Pforten der Hölle sollen sie nicht
 überwältigen. (Matth.16,18)

above:
Telegram of protest to National Chancellor Adolf Hitler.

center:
Handbill for the church election, 1933, written by Franz Hildebrandt.

below:
In front of a church door in Berlin: posters for the church election, July 23, 1933.

Church elections

Strong pressure from outside the church and internal disunity led von Bodelschwingh to give up the position of national bishop. Under the leadership of Ludwig Müller, the constitution of the German Protestant Church was then elaborated in a short space of time, and became state law on July 14. Surprisingly, church elections were called for July 23. Although there was little doubt that the German Christians would win, the young reformers had no option but to take part and to make the best of things. Bonhoeffer and Hildebrandt threw themselves into a hopeless election campaign.

Appeal to take part in the church election.

Handbills were produced during the weekend of July 15 and 16, but the Gestapo appeared on July 17 and confiscated both the handbills and the electoral lists. The German Christians succeeded in getting a court order prohibiting the "Protestant Church List" of candidates whom the young reformers had put forward. Bonhoeffer and Gerhard Jacobi went on July 18 to the Gestapo headquarters, where Jacobi's proposal of a new list called "Gospel and Church" was accepted.

The "Aryan paragraph" in the church

After their electoral success, the German Christians sought to have the "Aryan paragraph" adopted by the church too. In a leaflet written in August, Bonhoeffer spelled out the consequences: "The exclusion of Jewish Christians from the Christian community destroys the substance of the church."

On September 5, 1933, the general synod of the Old Prussian Church met in the former Upper Chamber in Berlin. The majority of the delegates wore the "brown garment of honor." They approved the "Church law regarding the Legal Situation of Clergy and Church officials," which stipulated that only one who "unreservedly supported the National Socialist state and the German Protestant church" and was of Aryan descent could become a clergyman. Before a vote was taken on the "Aryan paragraph," the church opposition, led by Martin Niemöller, left the chamber in protest.

In the aftermath of the "brown synod," Bonhoeffer asked Karl Barth in a letter of September 9 whether he believed it possible "to remain in a church which has ceased to be a Christian church, or to continue to exercise a parochial ministry which has become a privilege for Aryans." Barth replied: " ... I too believe that the *status confessionis* now exists." Nevertheless, he recommended that Bonhoeffer wait until "the collision takes place at an even more central point." But what could be "an even more central point" than the Aryan paragraph?

above:
Old Prussian general synod, September 5, 1933. At the front of the picture: President Koch, the leader of the "young reformers'" group. In the center, General Superintendent Otto Dibelius, who had been dismissed from his post.

below:
Letter to Karl Barth, September 9, 1933 (excerpt).

Lieber Herr Professor!

In Ihrer Schrift haben Sie gesagt, daß dort, wo eine Kirche den Arierparagraphen einführen würde, sie aufhört christliche Kirche zu sein. In dieser Meinung ist sich ein großer Teil hiesiger Pfarrer mit Ihnen einig. Nun ist das zu Erwartende eingetreten, und ich bitte Sie im Namen vieler Freunde, Pfarrer und Studenten darum, uns wissen zu lassen, ob Sie es für eine Möglichkeite halten, in einer Kirche, die aufgehört hat, christliche Kirche zu sein, zu bleiben, beziehungsweise ein Pfarramt, das zu einem Privileg für Arier geworden ist, weiter zu verwalten. Wir haben zunächst eine Erklärung aufgesetzt, in der wir der Kirchenregierung mitteilen wollen, daß mit dem Arierparagraphen sich die evangelische Kirche der Altpreußischen Union von der Kirche Christi getrennt hat und wollen die Antwort darauf abwarten, d.h. ob die unterzeichneten Pfarrer entlassen werden oder ob man sich etwas derartiges unbekümmert sagen läßt. Mehreren unter uns liegt jetzt der Gedanke der Freikirche sehr nahe. Der Unterschied zwischen unserer heutigen Situation und der Luthers liegt doch wohl darin, daß die katholische Kirche Luther unter Bezeichnung der häretischen Sätze ausstieß, daß aber unser Kirchenregiment das nicht kann, weil ihm der Begriff des Häretischen überhaupt gänzlich fehlt. Darum läßt sich auch nicht einfach von Luthers Haltung her argumentieren. Ich weiß, daß jetzt viele auf Ihr Urteil warten, weiß auch daß die meisten der Ansicht sind, Sie würden dazu raten zu bleiben bis man herausgetan wird. Nun sind aber schon welche herausgetan, nämlich die Juden-Christen und anderen wird sehr bald unter Angabe völlig unkirchlicher Gründe dasselbe geschehen. Was folgt daraus für uns, wenn die Kirche wirklich nicht nur jeweils einzelne Gemeinde ist, wie steht es mit der Solidarität der Pfarrer untereinander, wann gibt es überhaupt eine Möglichkeit des Austritts aus der Kirche? Daß der status confessionis da ist, daran kann ja nicht gezweifelt werden, aber worin sich die confessio heute am sachgemäßesten ausdrückt, darüber sind wir uns nicht im klaren.

Gleichzeitig erlaube ich mir, Ihnen einen Durchschlag ei-

Verpflichtung.

1. Ich verpflichte mich, mein Amt als Diener des Wortes auszurichten allein in der Bindung an die Hl.Schrift und an die Bekenntnisse der Reformation als die rechte Auslegung der Hl.Schrift.

2. Ich verpflichte mich, gegen alle Verletzung solchen Bekenntnisstandes mit rückhaltlosem Einsatz zu protestieren.

4. Ich weiß mich nach bestem Vermögen mit verantwortlich für die, die um solchen Bekenntnisstandes willen verfolgt werden.

5. In solcher Verpflichtung bezeuge ich, daß eine Verletzung des Bekenntnisstandes mit der Anwendung des Arierparagraphen im Raum der Kirche Christi geschaffen ist.

...............,den..........1933
(Genaue Ortsangabe)

....
(Unterschrift)

Vermerk: Der Punkt 3 der früheren Verpflichtungsformulare fällt fort.

above:
Declaration of the obligations assumed by pastors or members of the Emergency Association of Pastors.

left:
Pastor Martin Niemöller, 1936.

Emergency Association of Pastors

At the end of September, Martin Niemöller founded the "Emergency Association of Pastors" which grew out of a letter of protest he had written together with Bonhoeffer:

According to our church's confession of faith, the ecclesiastical teaching office depends only on the appropriate call to exercise it. The "Aryan paragraph" of the new law for church officials creates a law which contradicts this fundamental proposition of our confession, thereby proclaiming as church law a situation which must be considered – in the light of our confession – as unjust and an infringement of the confession of faith.

There can be no doubt that those clergymen affected by this law regarding church officials, unless a due procedure has deprived them of the rights pertaining to the clerical state, continue to enjoy the full right to preach the Word freely and to administer freely the sacraments in the Protestant church of the Old Prussian union, which is founded on the confessions of faith of the Reformation.

Anyone who assents to such a breach of the confession of faith automatically excludes himself from the fellowship of the church. We demand therefore that this law, which separates the Protestant church of the Old Prussian union from the Christian church, be abrogated immediately.

To these three points made by Bonhoeffer and Niemöller, we need only add that they promised their help to those in the church who were affected by the "Aryan paragraph."

Assembly of the World Federation in Sofia and the Wittenberg National Synod

From September 15 to 20, 1933, the World Alliance for Promoting International Friendship through the Churches met in Sofia. It affirmed in its concluding resolution:

... Above all, we deplore the fact that the measures taken by the state against Jews in Germany have had such an effect on public opinion that many groups hold the Jewish race to be inferior. We protest against the decision of the Prussian general synod and of other synods to apply to the church the Aryan paragraph of the state, thereby imposing considerable restrictions on pastors and church officials who are not in fact Aryan by birth. We regard this as a denial of the explicit doctrine and of the spirit of the Gospel of Jesus Christ.

Unaffected by this, the National Synod met in Wittenberg on September 27, to elect Ludwig Müller as national bishop. Early on this lovely fall day, Bonhoeffer was brought by his parents' chauffeur to Luther's former university town. He was accompanied in the car by Gertrud Staewen and Franz Hildebrandt; in the baggage compartment were packets of the leaflet "To the National Synod."

In the city church of Wittenberg, above Luther's tomb, Hossenfelder cried out: "My national bishop, I salute you!" And Hildebrandt whispered to Bonhoeffer that he now believed in the doctrine of the "real rotation" of Luther's bones in his grave ...

above:
Session of the expanded Executive Committee of the World Federation, September 15-20, 1933, in Sofia (D. Bonhoeffer second from right).

center:
National Synod in Wittenberg, September 27, 1933. Center (from left to right): President Koopmann, Prof. Fezer, Bishop Müller, Bishop Schöffel, Prof. Schumann.

below:
Ludwig Müller, flanked by Nazi Party office-bearers, on the steps of the Council Chambers in Wittenberg.

An die Nationalsynode
der Deutschen Evangelischen Kirche zu Wittenberg.

Die Nationalsynode von Wittenberg soll einen neuen Abschnitt in der Geschichte unserer evangelischen Kirche einleiten. In dieser Stunde erheben wir im Namen von 2000 evangelischen Pfarrern unsere Stimme.

Die Nationalsynode darf nicht durch ihr feierliches Gepräge den Anschein einer geeinten Kirche erwecken, solange die Gemeinden von tiefsten Gegensätzen zerrissen sind. Die Aufreizung der Gegensätze sehen wir als ein Gericht Gottes über unsere Kirche an. Wir wissen uns mit hineingestellt in dieses Gericht und wollen es mit allen tragen, die sich mit uns unter den Spruch Gottes beugen, damit der Herr Christus sich uns wieder zuwenden möge.

Die Nationalsynode tagt an der Stätte, an der Luther in seinen Invocavit-Predigten gegen die Verkehrung der Kirche Christi in falsches Wesen vom Evangelium her Einspruch erhoben hat. So dürfen wir erwarten, daß nicht alle Synodalen zu den heute umkämpften Fragen mutlos schweigen, zumal wir wissen, daß manche unter ihnen genau wie wir in ihrem Gewissen beschwert sind. Und wenn keiner von ihnen den Mut aufbringt, so fordern wir von den lutherischen Bischöfen, besonders von dem künftigen Reichsbischof, daß sie um der Wahrheit willen ein klares Wort sagen. Die Kirche darf auf ihrer ersten Nationalsynode sich nicht nur mit Worten zum Evangelium bekennen, sondern muß mit der Tat die ihr auferlegten Fragen evangeliumgemäß entscheiden.

Damit die Kirche nicht mit einer verborgenen Schuld ihren Weg beginnt, erklären wir um der Wahrheit und der Liebe willen Folgendes:

1. Die Art und Weise, in der neue Ordnungen in der Kirche eingeführt wurden und angewandt werden, hat schwere innere Not über ungezählte ernste Christen gebracht. Auf entscheidend wichtigen Synoden hat die jetzige Mehrheit den Vertretern der Minderheit die gründliche Beratung und freie Aussprache versagt, auch bei Fragen, die das innerste Wesen der Kirche und ihren Auftrag berühren. Das kirchliche Leben steht seit einigen Monaten unter dem Druck der Gewalt einer kirchlichen Gruppe. Es darf aber nicht sein, daß die Kirche Jesu Christi unter Verleugnung der brüderlichen Liebe durch Herrschaft der Gewalt zu einem Reich dieser Welt wird.

2. Unter stillschweigender Billigung des neuen Kirchenregiments sind auf landeskirchlichen Synoden Gesetze beschlossen und in Kraft gesetzt, die mit der Heiligen Schrift und dem Bekenntnis der Kirche im Widerspruch stehen. Hier ist insbesondere der Arierparagraph zu nennen. Wir stellen fest, daß mit der landeskirchlichen Einführung solcher Gesetze der Reichsgesetzgebung der deutschen Kirche vorgegriffen ist, und fordern von der Nationalsynode, daß sie ihre Vollmachten nicht anderen Instanzen abgibt, sondern selber derartige bekenntniswidrige landeskirchliche Gesetze aufhebt. Es darf nicht sein, daß das Evangelium durch menschliche Gesetze begrenzt oder gar außer Kraft gesetzt wird.

3. Das kirchliche Amt ist in höchstem Maße dadurch gefährdet, daß Pfarrer und Kirchenbeamte deswegen verfolgt werden, weil sie in der in der Kirche zur Zeit herrschenden Gruppe nicht zu folgen vermögen. Hierdurch wird das Amt in einem Maße menschlichem Druck unterworfen, daß die Diener des Wortes in Gefahr stehen, das Gebot: „Man muß Gott mehr gehorchen als den Menschen!" zu verletzen und Menschenknechte zu werden. Wir fordern von der Nationalsynode, daß sie durch klare Beschlüsse die volle Freiheit der evangelischen Verkündigung und ihrer Träger sicherstellt. Es darf nicht sein, daß sich die kirchliche Verkündigung menschlichen Ansprüchen beugt.

In dieser ernsten Stunde, da wir aus schwerer Gewissensnot diesen Protest aussprechen müssen, geloben wir vor Gott, alle unsere Kräfte daran zu setzen, daß die Heilsbotschaft rein und lauter unter uns verkündet werde als die Offenbarung des lebendigen Gottes in Christus.

Wir geloben, diesen unseren Auftrag als Diener des Wortes allein in der Bindung an die Heilige Schrift nach dem in den Bekenntnisschriften gewiesenen Verständnis auszurichten.

Wir geloben, in unserer Kirche dem Geist der Wahrheit und der Liebe nach bestem Vermögen Raum zu schaffen, aller Unwahrheit und Lieblosigkeit offen zu begegnen und durch unsern Dienst als Seelsorger für uns und unsere Gemeinden die Bruderschaft derer zu verwirklichen, die Christus angehören.

Wir werden also nicht aufhören, all das zu bekämpfen, was die Kirche in ihrem Wesen zerstört.

Wir werden nicht aufhören, gegen jede Verletzung des Bekenntnisses laut und weithin vernehmlich Einspruch zu erheben.

Wir werden nicht aufhören, in treuem Gehorsam gegen unser Ordinationsgelübde unbeirrt am Aufbau der Deutschen Evangelischen Kirche zu arbeiten.

Wir vertrauen dem Herrn der Kirche und bitten ihn, er möchte unserer Kirche neues Leben aus seinem Geist und seinen Frieden schenken!

Berlin, den 27. September 1933.

Bonhoeffer Burckhardt Figur Fricke Grüneisen Hildebrand Hildebrandt Hitzigrath Jacobi Eduard Lindenmeyer Friedrich Lindenmeyer Link Messow Moldaenke Müller-Dahlem Niemöller Petersen Praetorius Puttkammer Schwebel Stupperich Wendland-Steglitz.

Leaflet "To the National Synod."

London
(1933–34)

The conflicts in the first six months of 1933 led Dietrich Bonhoeffer into realms far beyond the field of his activity hitherto. At the same time, it had become obvious that his views were very different from those who fought alongside him: they did not accept his idea of an "interdict," i.e., the refusal to carry out official acts such as marriages and funerals, when Bonhoeffer proposed this as the appropriate response to the "Aryan paragraph" of the state. On October 24, 1933, he wrote to Karl Barth: "I felt that I was in a radical opposition to all my friends – an incomprehensible situation. And so I thought that the time had come to spend a period in the wilderness." This is the time of preparation: Bonhoeffer knew that the church opposition, in whose work he shared, "is only a very transitory intermediary stage, before a very different opposition comes ... And I believe that all of Christendom must join us in praying that the 'resistance unto the shedding of our blood' may come, and that there may be found persons willing to endure this."

On November 12, 1933, he was unanimously elected pastor by the United parish in Sydenham and the Reformed St. Paul's parish. This meant that he took over the administration of two of the six German parishes in London. Their autonomy and their small dimensions recall the situation in the Free churches. Earlier, each had had its own pastor and organist, but after the First World War, some of them – e.g., Sydenham and St. Paul's – were forced to take the decision to amalgamate and to hire one shared clergyman.

Sydenham-Forest Hill, founded in 1875, consisted mostly of well-to-do merchants. German diplomats, who lived before the First World War on Forest Hill, also belonged to this parish. During Bonhoeffer's ministry, the chancellor of the German embassy, Theodor Lang, lived there. He obtained important political information for Bonhoeffer and helped him in the aid he gave to German refugees.

above:
Letter of D. Bonhoeffer to Consistorial Counselor Heckel, October 4, 1933.

left:
Memorandum about sending Bonhoeffer to London (October 6).

center right:
Bonhoeffer's church in London, Dacres Road, Sydenham (photograph 1934).

Jahresbericht
1933/34.

Phil. 1, 18: „. . . . dass nur Christus verkündigt werde."

Was spielen alle Veränderungen, die das Leben einer Gemeinde mit sich bringt, für eine Rolle gegenüber dem einen schlechthin Unveränderlichen „. . . . dass nur Christus verkündigt werde"? Ein Pfarrer ist gegangen, ein anderer ist gekommen — was liegt daran angesichts dessen, dass sie ja beide nichts für sich sind, sondern Botschafter desselben einen Herren und Reiches, dass es ja so oder so nur darum geht, dass der ewige Auftrag ausgerichtet werde, „dass nur Christus verkündigt werde". Individualität, Sympathie, Antipathie hin und her — hier in der Gemeinde Jesu Christi geht es wirklich um Wichtigeres, Grösseres, Dringlicheres — nicht um den Pfarrer, sondern um Christus, „dass nur Christus verkündigt werde" — hier gibt es nicht mehr Neigung und Abneigung, sondern Glaube und Unglaube — das ist die bange Wahl.

Wir leben in einer Zeit, die sich von Illusionen verschiedenster Art befreit. Auch die Kirche darf sich nicht länger Illusionen hingeben. Es geht auch in ihr um das Ganze. Sie muss wissen, mit wem sie zu rechnen hat und mit wem nicht. Besser eine kleine einsatzbereite Truppe als ein grosses Heer, das mit Deserteuren durchsetzt ist. Das gilt auch für die Kirche. Es geht um Glauben und Unglauben, um Gehorsam oder Ungehorsam, um Nachfolgen oder Desertieren, um Christus oder die Götzen unseres Lebens.

Die Tage sind vorüber, in denen man Zeit zu haben glaubte, auf der Kanzel ein erbauliches Allerlei von Literatur, Weltanschauung, Lebensweise, Politik bringen zu können. Die Zeit der Kirche ist knapp bemessen. Wer weiss, ob das, was heute nicht gesagt und gehört wird, morgen nicht schon zu spät kommt. Es ist Entscheidungszeit.

above left:
German Reformed St. Paul's church, which was bombed during World War II (photograph 1936).

above right:
Pastor Dr. Julius Rieger.

center:
Bonhoeffer's residence in London: Parish house, 23 Manor Mount, Forest Hill, London S.E. 23. His apartment was on the second floor: the first and second windows from the left are his dining room; then the window of his study; then the guest room. The parish hall was on the first floor. The sacristan's apartment was in the basement.

below:
Annual report of the Sydenham parish for 1933/34, presented in the name of the parish council by D. Bonhoeffer (excerpt).

St Paul's, the other parish, followed the Reformed confession and lay in London's East End. Its members included craftsmen's families who had come from Germany, butchers, bakers, and tailors, mostly from Württemberg. At this point, English was the only language most of them spoke. They had suffered great hostility as Germans during the First World War, and some had had to close their businesses. Now they lent a ready ear to Bonhoeffer's appeals to help those who emigrated from Germany.

Bonhoeffer's election had to be confirmed by the Foreign Office of the German Protestant church. To begin with, he delayed in asking for this confirmation; later, he simply stopped answering letters on this subject. Bonhoeffer wanted to avoid official recognition by the leadership of the German national church. This meant that he risked losing his pension rights and provision for his old age.

On October 17, 1933, Bonhoeffer moved into the German parish house in the South London suburb of Forest Hill. The house is on the southern slope of a hill, at the foot of the well-tended Horniman Park, with a vista of row upon row of houses stretching to Kent and Surrey on the horizon. To the north, one standing in the Park can see the city, Parliament, St. Paul's cathedral, and the harbor as far as the hills of Hampstead and Finsbury Park.

Bonhoeffer furnished his first-floor apartment with furniture from his home, including his huge Beckstein piano. Franz Hildebrandt spent several months there. Herbert Jehle, Bonhoeffer's pacifist friend, visited him from Cambridge. Here Bonhoeffer gathered youth groups and musical circles for Christmas plays and church music, for trios and quartets. Bonhoeffer and Hildebrandt became good friends of Dr. Julius Rieger, a pastor who worked in East London.

Struggle against the National Church leadership

In a mass rally of the German Christians in the Sport Palace in Berlin on November 13, 1933, Dr. Krause, the director of the Berlin district, demanded "that a German people's church take seriously the proclamation of the simple Good News, purified of every oriental attitude, and of a heroic Jesus-figure who is the basis of a Christianity appropriate to our race." Krause continued that the German Christians wanted a "liberation from the Old Testament with its Jewish morality based on rewards, a liberation from these tales of cattle-dealers and pimps." This led to protests; many people left the church.

Five weeks later, the national bishop, acting on his own authority, put his signature to the contract which incorporated the Protestant Youth movement into the Hitler Youth. This was followed by the "muzzling decree" of January 4, 1934, in which Ludwig Müller forbade any mention of the church conflicts in ecclesiastical buildings and publications and threatened that disobedience of this order would be punished by dismissal from office. The Emergency Association of Pastors issued an appeal to disobey the "muzzling decree." The pastors in London reacted at once: on January 7, they sent the following telegram to the leadership of the National Church: FOR THE SAKE OF THE GOSPEL AND OF OUR CONSCIENCE WE ADHERE TO THE DECLARATION OF THE EMERGENCY ASSOCIATION AND WITHHOLD OUR CONFIDENCE FROM NATIONAL BISHOP MÜLLER. GERMAN PASTORS IN LONDON WEHRHAN. In his draft, Bonhoeffer had written: "no longer recognize the national bishop."

"As long as national bishop Müller remains in office, there remains the risk that we may secede," wrote the London pastors to Federal President von Hindenburg on January 15, 1934. Bonhoeffer encouraged the bishop of Chichester to write to Hindenburg, as the "member at the head" of the Protestant church. In this situation, the heads of those federal-state churches which were still intact (Bishop Marahrens in Hanover; Bishop Wurm in Württemberg; and Bishop Meiser in Bavaria) and who had kept their distance from the national church postponed the secession which

Der Reichsbischof richtet das Christentum aus

above:
Meeting of the German Christians in the Sport Palace on November 13, 1933 (1st from left: Dr. Krause, director of the Berlin district; 6th from left: Dr. Werner, president of the Supreme Church Council).

left:
Photomontage by John Heartfield: the national bishop organizes Christendom (1934).

below:
From left: Federal-state bishops Wurm, Stuttgart; Marahrens, Hanover; Meiser, Munich (before a discussion with Hitler in Berlin, October 30, 1934).

Berlin-Dahlem, den 31.Januar 1934

An den Herrn Reichsbischof
Berlin.

Der Pfarrernotbund sieht sich veranlaßt, im Namen mehrer tausend Pfarrer zu erklären, daß wir uns um unseres in Gottes Wort gebundenen Gewissens willen nicht in der Lage sehen, irgendwie von unserem Urteil über die Bekenntniswidrigkeit der beanstandeten Gesetze und Verordnungen sowie über die Evangeliumswidrigkeit des darauf ge gründeten Gewalthandelns im Raum der Kirche Jesu Christi abzugehen.
Wir haben auch weiterhin die Pflicht und nehmen infolgedessen auch das Recht für uns in Anspruch gegen alle Verletzungen des Bekenntnisses in Lehre und Gesetzgebung der Kirche und gegen alle Maßnahmen, die gegen den Geist des Evangeliums verstoßen, Protest zu erheben.
Wir erklären noch einmal, daß es für uns bei der Neuregelung der Kirche und ihres Regiments nicht um eine Frage der Macht, sondern um die evangelische Wahrheit geht, und wir beschwören die in der Kirche herrschenden Männer, diese Tatsache in ihrem ganzen tiefen Ernst zu sehen.

In Auftrag: gez.Niemöller, Pfarrer.

above:
Letter of protest by the Emergency Association of Pastors to National Bishop Müller, signed by M. Niemöller.

center:
Consistorial Counselor T. Heckel, appointed bishop and head of the Church Office for Foreign Affairs in 1934.

below:
D. Bonhoeffer's copy of the minutes of the discussions of the German Protestant pastors in Great Britain with Dr. Heckel on February 9,

PROTOKOLL der Besprechungen der deutschen evangelischen Pastoren Grossbritanniens mit Oberkreisторialrat Dr. HECKEL.
9/8/34

Nachstehende Punkte sind die Basis, auf der die hiesigen Gemeinden bereit sein würden, der neuen evangelischen Kirche beizutreten:

1) Die evangelische Kirche steht auf dem Boden der Reformation.
2) Sie gründet sich auf die Heilige Schrift Alten und Neuen Testaments.
3) Den Arier-Paragraphen erkennen die deutsch-evangelischen Pastoren Grossbritanniens **nicht** an und erwarten von der Reichskirche, dass dieser Paragraph nirgends durchgeführt wird.
4) Die deutsche Reichskirche setzt keine Pfarrer in Deutschland ab, die obige Punkte anerkennen, es sei denn wegen anderer, schwer wiegender Disziplinarübertretungen.
5) Die Pfarrer erklären, dass sie durch die Auflösung des Kirchenbundes nicht mehr an die Reichskirche gebunden sind, dass sie aber dennoch bereit sind, auf vorstehender Basis in christlicher Liebe und Gemeinschaft bei der Reichskirche zu bleiben.
6) Die deutsch-evangelischen Kirchen Grossbritanniens, die sich bereit erklären, der neuen Reichskirche angegliedert zu sein, erklären aber ausdrücklich, dass sie, wie jetzt bestehend, jederzeit das Recht haben, aus diesem Kirchenverbande wieder auszutreten.

LONDON, den 9. Februar 1934.

they had threatened, and made a "truce" with the national bishop until they should be received by Hitler. This meeting was often postponed, but finally took place on January 25. For a time, the opposition hoped that this encounter would lead to Müller's dismissal, but this did not happen: on the contrary, the church leaders (including Wurm, Meiser, and Marahrens) declared, "under the impression of the great historical hour": "The assembled church leaders are united in their support of the national bishop and are willing to implement the measures and ordinances he promulgates in the sense in which he intends them."

The English press paid great attention to these conflicts in the church in Germany. This induced the leadership of the National Church to endeavor to pacify the foreign press, and they warned the German Protestant pastors in London to avoid thoughtless contacts with ecumenical circles and with the world press. Against this background, the Consistorial Counselor, Dr. Heckel, announced his visit. A few days before this, Martin Niemöller had been suspended from his office as pastor. The London pastors made careful preparations for this unwanted visitation. They listed six points as "the basis on which our communities would be willing to join the new Protestant church." Heckel, however, demanded a declaration of loyalty to the national bishop; the memorandum of the pastors was rejected.

While explaining the declaration of loyalty that he had prepared for them to sign, Heckel linked the opposition with examples of treasonable activities in Germany. This prompted pastors Bonhoeffer, Rieger, and Steiniger to leave the room in protest. The conference ended without any definitive agreement.

Bonhoeffer and Bishop Bell

When Heckel, now a bishop and head of the "Church Office for Foreign Affairs," demanded that Bonhoeffer – in the interests of both of them – should abstain "henceforth from all ecumenical activity," Bonhoeffer refused, since he intended to pursue his "purely ecclesiastical and theological ecumenical work." Bonhoeffer did his utmost to persuade his ecumenical contacts to break off relations with the leadership of the National Church: "Confession – that is the word on our lips in Germany today. Confession is also the word for the ecumenical movement. Let us have done with fear of this word! The cause of Christ itself is at stake. Do we want to be found asleep?" (Letter to general secretary Henry Louis Henriod, April 7, 1934).

Bonhoeffer had met the bishop of Chichester, George K.A. Bell, at an ecumenical meeting in Geneva in the summer of 1932. Now he urged him to break with the leadership of the National Church, in the name of the ecumenical movement. On May 10, 1934, the ecumenical pastoral letter of the chairman of the Council was published: "A Message regarding the German Evangelical Church to the Representatives of the Churches on the Universal Council for Life and Work from the Bishop of Chichester." The main reason for the anxieties of the Christian church outside Germany "is that the national bishop, in the name of the 'Führer principle,' has exercised an autocratic authority which is not moderated by additional or traditional limitations, and is without precedent in the history of the church." The initiative Bonhoeffer took, and his help in the drafting of this pastoral letter, were his contribution to the Barmen synod, which met three weeks later.

above:
George K. A. Bell (1883–1958), Lord Bishop of Chichester.

below:
Letter by Bishop Bell to the editor of the Times, March 19, 1934 (published in the periodical Junge Kirche 8/1934).

Auslandsdeutsche Gemeinden und ökumenische Bewegung

„An den Herrn Herausgeber der ‚Times'. Sehr geehrter Herr, ich werde von verschiedenen Seiten, die eng mit der Deutschen Evangelischen Kirche in Verbindung stehen, unterrichtet, daß die kurze Notiz über meine Auseinandersetzung im vergangenen Monat mit den Repräsentanten der Deutschen Evangelischen Kirche in London, die Sie freundlichst veröffentlichten, ziemlich weit mißdeutet wurde. Es scheint, daß die Notiz, die eine allgemeine Studie ‚über verschiedene aktuelle Probleme in den Kirchen' empfahl, in Deutschland weitgehend als Beweis benutzt wurde, daß das Verhältnis zwischen der Deutschen Evangelischen Kirche und anderen Kirchen, repräsentiert durch den Ökumenischen Rat für praktisches Christentum, völlig ungetrübt sei. Deshalb soll sehr eindeutig und klar festgestellt werden, daß eine solche Folgerung nicht gezogen werden darf. Im Laufe dieser Verhandlungen übergab ich den Delegierten eine Aufstellung solcher ungelöster Fragen, die außer dem Arier-Paragraphen in anderen Kirchen Mißfallen verursachten. Unter diesen Punkten waren u. a. folgende:

Die Entlassung von Pastoren wegen ihrer Opposition gegenüber einer deutsch-christlichen Politik.

Die Tatsache, daß politische Gesichtspunkte über religiöse Gesichtspunkte, insbesondere über das Prinzip der Bekenntnisfreiheit gestellt werden.

Die ernste Gefahr, daß die Kirche als Instrument der Nationalsozialistischen Partei benutzt wird und vom Staat verschluckt wird.

Diese und andere Punkte rufen immer noch, trotz aller seitdem geführten Korrespondenz, die schwersten Befürchtungen hervor. Der Protest in meinem Brief an den Reichsbischof, vom Verwaltungsrat des Ökumenischen Rates gutgeheißen, ist nicht inzwischen etwa gemildert worden. Im Gegenteil, der Reichsbischof hat durch seine kürzliche Rede bei einer Versammlung der Deutschen Christen im Sportpalast und durch seine Gesetze und Verordnungen schwerwiegende Gründe für eine Verschärfung des Protestes gegeben. In der Rede im Sportpalast soll er, wie sowohl in der deutschen wie in der ausländischen Presse berichtet wird, gesagt haben, daß er nicht eher ruhen würde, bevor nicht jede Kanzel ihren ‚deutschchristlichen' Pastor habe und alle Kirchenstühle besetzt seien mit Deutschen Christen. Seine jüngsten Maßnahmen unter der Mitwirkung von Bischof Oberheid, von einer unaufhörlichen Reihe von Rücktritten und Suspensionen begleitet, müssen als aufeinanderfolgende Etappen in der Konzentration zu einer absoluten Autokratie in der Reichskirchenregierung betrachtet werden.

Die außerdeutschen Kirchen, besonders die, welche im Ökumenischen Rat vertreten sind, haben ein tiefes Verlangen nach brüderlichen Beziehungen und Freundschaft mit der Deutschen Evangelischen Kirche. Aber es kann nicht stark genug betont werden, daß, solange noch irgendeine Frage um die Anwendung des Arier-Paragraphen besteht, und solange derartige Zwangsmethoden in der Kirchenregierung angewandt werden, wie sie durch die augenblickliche Behandlung von Pastoren und Gemeindegliedern, die, obwohl durchaus loyal dem Deutschen Reich gegenüber eingestellt sind, gegen die jetzige Autokratie der Reichskirche aus geistlichen Gründen opponieren, bewiesen werden, die Beziehungen zwischen der Deutschen Evangelischen Kirche und den anderen Kirchen nicht völlig ungetrübt sein können.

Ihr ergebener   George Cicestr: The Palace, Chichester, March 19."

At the beginning of November 1934, the bishop invited him for the first time to a meal in his club, the Athenaeum. Three weeks later, Bonhoeffer visited Bell in his episcopal residence in Chichester. From now on, they frequently consulted one another. This involved more than agreement on the substantial issues involved: they made demands of one another that only a solid friendship could prompt and support.

At this period, Bonhoeffer (like Bell) dismissed the idea of influencing the German church struggle by means of an appeal to Hitler: "Hitler has very clearly demonstrated who he is, and the church must know with whom it has to reckon. Isaiah did not go to Sennacherib! ... Hitler should not and must not hear, he is hardened of heart. Precisely for this reason, he should compel us to hear – that is how things are ... It is we who are to be converted, not Hitler" (letter of September 11, 1934).

Like Dietrich Bonhoeffer, Bishop Bell had his birthday on February 4, and they exchanged congratulations each year. When this was no longer possible, Bell sent his greetings to Bonhoeffer's twin sister, who had emigrated. Later, Bonhoeffer asked an English fellow prisoner to communicate his last reported words to Bishop Bell: "This is the end, for me the beginning of life."

above:
Chicester, The Bishop's Palace.

below:
The Athenaeum, Bishop Bell's
club on the Mall, London.

Parish work and the misery of exile

In London, Bonhoeffer had his first direct encounter with the misery of exile. "In addition to my parish work ... I have countless visitors, mostly Jews, who know me from somewhere or other and want something from me." His main concern was for the first wave of refugees from Germany.

Members of the Eppstein and Cromwell families met in Bonhoeffer's house. The former government minister Gottfried W. Treviranus had his son confirmed by Bonhoeffer. In the summer of 1934, Bonhoeffer asked Reinhold Niebuhr in America for help for a number of persons, including the author Arnim T. Wegner, who had published an "Admonitory letter" to Hitler at Easter 1933.

above:
"Non-Aryan" emigrants board their ship.

below:
Letter by D. Bonhoeffer to Prof. Niebuhr, July 13, 1934.

Pfarrer D. Bonhoeffer
23, Manor Mount. S.E. 23   13. Juli 1934.

     Sehr verehrter, lieber Herr Professor!
Sie werden sich wundern von mir mal wieder zu hören nach
so langer Zeit. Das ist eigentlich schlimm; denn ich habe
es oft vorgehabt im letzten Jahr an Sie zu schreiben und
einmal Ihre Meinung zu den Dingen zu hören. Nun kam vor
einiger Zeit mein Vetter und hat mir viel von Ihnen er-
zählt; auch kam eine so liebenswürdige Einladung Ihrer
Frau Schwiegermutter, der ich leider nicht folgen konnte.
So sind in der letzten Zeit allerlei Fäden wieder zu Ihnen
hingelaufen. Dennoch ist es ein ganz besonderer Anlass,
aus dem ich Ihnen heute schreibe. Ich brauche Ihren Rat
und Ihre Hilfe in einigen Emigrantenangelegenheiten. Es it
ganz natürlich, dass ich ich mit den Dingen seit meinem
Aufenthalt in London sehr viel zu tun bekommen habe; nun
würde ich heute gern wissen, ob und in welcher Richtung
bei Ihnen drüben für Studenten (jüdische bzw. aus politi-
schen Gründen von der Universität relegierte) eine Ein-
richtung besteht, die ihnen entweder eine Fortsetzung des
Studiums oder Umschulung auf einen andern Beruf ermöglicht.
Es hat sich zwar hier kürzlich erst ein Komittee besonders
für Akademiker gegründet, aber die Mittel sind gleich Null.
Hier in London liegt mir besonders auf der Seele ein Mann,
33 Jahre, ehemaliger Führer des Republikanischen Studenten-

bundes , Jurist, der in wirklicher Bedrängnis ist und den
ich nirgends unterbringen kann. Er ist glaube ich kein beson-
deres Licht, aber es muss ihm einfach geholfen werden. Nun
hätte ich gern gewusst, ob in denStaaten die Möglichkeit
bestünde, dass er sein Studium fortsetzt oder was neues an-
fängt, vielleicht ein Stipendium oder soetwas. Das ist der
eine Fall. - Der andere ist der Schriftsteller Arnim T. Wegner - Tillich wird ihn sicher kennen - sehr linksgerichtet,
furchtbare Zeit im Konzentrationslager und völlig kaputt.Er
hat hier nichts finden können und ist verzweifelt dran. -
Verzeihen Sie, wenn ich Sie mit diesen Dingen bemühe, aber
es ist nur ein winziger Ausschnitt von dem, was wir hier
fast täglich zu sehen bekommen, und wo man dann schliesslich
auch einfach dasteht und nicht mehr helfen kann.Meine Gemeinden unterstützen mich inder Arbeit sehr verständnisvoll.
Das ist eine bedeutende Hilfe. -
Die letzten Ereignisse in Deutschland haben ja nun unzweideu-
tig gezeigt, wohin die Fahrt geht. Es hat mich nur gewundert,
dass unter den Erschossenen vom 30. juni kein evangelischer
Pfarrer war. Man beginnt in unseren Kreisen mehr und mehr zu
verstehen, - besonders nach dem letzten Maulkorberlass von
Frick, dass die Kulturkampfsituation da ist. Es ist sehr selt
sam zu sehen, wie lange es dauert, ehe ein evangelischer Pfar
rer das überhaupt für möglich hält. Auch heute will man noch
in Westfalen sehr viel weniger davon wissen als etwa bei uns

left:
Letter by Willy Rosenstein to Dietrich Bonhoeffer, March 20, 1934.

below:
The government bench in parliament (then sitting in the Kroll Opera) during Hitler's account of "Röhm's coup d'état." From left: Goebbels, Milch, Darré, von Eltz-Rübenach, von Blomberg, Gürtner, Seldte. In the background (4th from left): Bonhoeffer's brother-in-law Hans von Dohnanyi, personal assistant to the National Minister for Justice, Gürtner, since 1929.

On June 30, 1934, the so-called Röhm rebellion was bloodily suppressed in Germany. In his address to Parliament, giving an account of the measures he had taken, Hitler spoke of 77 victims; Bonhoeffer's brother-in-law, Hans Dohnanyi, told him a different story, according to the diary of Julius Rieger: "Bonhoeffer's source in the Ministry of Justice has told him that 207 persons were shot on June 30 and July 1." On the Sunday after the bloodbath of the Röhm rebellion, Bonhoeffer preached in his London parish about the "tower of Siloam" (Luke 13:1-5), the narrative of a murder in antiquity. Unsparingly, he confronted the community with Jesus' summons to repentance: "Unless you repent, you will all likewise perish … This is when things get dangerous. Now we are no longer onlookers, observers, judges of these events. Now it is we ourselves who are being addressed, it is we who are affected. This happened for us. It is to us that God is speaking. It is we who are meant."

He wrote to Erwin Sutz on September 11, 1934: "We must finally stop appealing to theology to justify our reserved silence about what the state is doing – for that is nothing but fear. 'Open your mouth for the one who is voiceless' – for who in the church today still remembers that that is the least of the Bible's demands in times such as these?"

Ecumenism and the German Protestant Church

As youth secretary of the World Alliance for Promoting International Friendship through the Churches, Bonhoeffer had the task of preparing the Ecumenical Youth Conference which was planned for August 1934, parallel to the assembly of the World Alliance, on the Danish island of Fanö. En route to Fanö, he met Hans Bernd von Haeften, who had been confirmed along with him. Eight years later, Hans Bernd's brother Werner was to ask Dietrich: "I can enter the Führer's headquarters with my gun. Should I shoot him?" Von Haeften made his decision: as adjutant to Colonel von Stauffenberg, he died with him on the evening of July 20, 1944, in the Bendlerstraße.

Hans-Bernd (left) and Werner v. Haeften, ca. 1925.

In May 1934, the Barmen Confessional Synod had condemned the theology of the German Christians as heresy. For Bonhoeffer, this resolution had consequences: his attendance in Fanö depended in part on the question "whether representatives of the present leadership of the National Church take part in the conference. At any rate, the members of our delegation have agreed that they will not attend those meetings in Fanö at which representatives of the church leadership are present. It would be good if this alternative were clearly seen by everyone. And I hope that you too will help us to make it clear in good time which of the two 'churches' in Germany is supported by the ecumenical movement" (letter to T. de Félice, July 4, 1934).

Since, however, the statutes of the World Alliance made it impossible to accommodate the claim of the Confessing Church (as the alternative to the National Church was called) to be the legitimate German Protestant church, Bonhoeffer

WELTBUND FUER INTERNATIONALE FREUNDSCHAFTSARBEIT DER KIRCHEN.

ARBEITSAUSSCHUSS
Fanö, Dänemark, 24. August 1934

T a g e s o r d n u n g

1. Kurze Besprechung der letzten Zusammenkunft in Genf 1932

2. Todesfälle

3. Wahl der Ausschüsse
    a. Finanzen
    b. Executive
    c. Beisitzer der Arbeitsausschüsse
    d. Geschäftsführer : Vorschlag die Wahlen um ein Jahr
       zu verschieben
    e. Kommissionen

4. Finanzen :
    a. Darlegung der heutigen finanziellen Lage
       (Schriftwerk A)
    b. Budget für 1935 (Schriftwerk B)
    c. Bericht über den Stand des Gesammtvermögens
       (Schriftwerk C)
    d. Internationale Sekretäre

5. Entschluss über "Das Zeugnis der Kirche in der heutigen Weltlage", Vorschlag der britischen Vereinigung (Schriftwerk D).

6. Entschluss der Hauptversammlung der Kirche von Schottland vom 29. Mai 1934, vorgelegt von der britischen Vereinigung (Schriftwerk E)

7. Assyrische Christen.

above:
Conference program.

below:
During the Fanö conference: D. Bonhoeffer, R. Matsuda (Japan), J. Lasserre (France).

Entschliessungen zur kirchlichen Lage in Deutschland.

I. Der Oekumenische Rat für Praktisches Christentum hat in seiner Sitzung von Fanö, 24.—30. August nach gemeinsamem Gebet und Erörterung von Problemen, vor die die Kirche in der gesamten Welt gestellt ist, beschlossen, die Kirchen aufzufordern, während der nächsten Jahre in ökumenischer Zusammenarbeit und Gemeinschaft eine Neubesinnung über die Probleme der Beziehungen zwischen Kirche, Staat und Volk im Lichte der Grundanschauungen des christlichen Glaubens zu unternehmen.

II. Die Vertreter der Kirchen in vielen Ländern haben ihrer schweren Besorgnis Ausdruck gegeben, dass entscheidende Grundsätze der christlichen Freiheit im Leben der Deutschen Evangelischen Kirche gegenwärtig gefährdet oder in Frage gestellt seien.

Der Oekumenische Rat ist der Ueberzeugung, dass es die besondere Aufgabe der ökumenischen Bewegung ist, das Bewusstsein gegenseitiger Verantwortung in allen Teilen der Kirche Christi zum Ausdruck zu bringen und zu vertiefen.

Erfüllt von aufrichtig-herzlicher Gesinnung gegenüber dem deutschen Volke ...

gibt der Oekumenische Rat seiner Ueberzeugung Ausdruck, dass ein autokratisches Kirchenregiment, besonders wenn es durch feierlichen Eid dem Gewissen auferlegt wird, die Anwendung von Gewaltmethoden und die Unterdrückung freier Aussprache mit dem wahren Wesen der Kirche Christi unvereinbar sind und erbittet im Namen des Evangeliums für seine christlichen Brüder in der Deutschen Evangelischen Kirche

Freiheit, das Evangelium unseres Herrn Jesu Christi zu verkündigen und Seinem Wort gemäss zu leben,

Freiheit des gedruckten Wortes und der Versammlung im Dienste der christlichen Gemeinde,

Freiheit für die Kirche, die Jugend nach den Grundsätzen des christlichen Glaubens zu erziehen und sie vor Aufzwingung einer mit dem christlichen Glauben im Widerstreit stehenden Weltanschauung zu schützen.

III. Der Oekumenische Rat billigt die Schritte, die sein Präsident Lord Bischof von Chichester in seinem Namen unternommen hat.

Erklärung der deutschen Delegation.

I.

Die deutsche Delegation ist dankbar für den Geist der Brüderlichkeit, der während der diesjährigen Tagung des Oekumenischen Rates in Fanö weithin bewiesen wurde. Sie erkennt auch dankbar an, dass in der vorliegenden Resolution der ernsthafte Versuch gemacht ist, verständnis- und verantwortungsvoll zu reden und die deutsche Kirche in ihrem Kampf der ökumenischen Verbundenheit des Glaubens zu versichern.

Trotzdem sieht sich die deutsche Delegation nicht in der Lage, der vorliegenden Resolution zuzustimmen. Sie gibt vielmehr noch einmal ihrer schon wiederholt ausgesprochenen Meinung Ausdruck, dass öffentliche Resolutionen der inneren kirchlichen Entwicklung in Deutschland nicht förderlich sind. Wir sind der Ueberzeugung, dass der Oekumenische Rat um der Zukunft der ökumenischen Bewegung willen mit besonderer Verantwortung der Grenzen seiner ökumenischen Aufgabe im Verhältnis zu den inneren Angelegenheiten einer Mitgliedskirche bewusst sein muss...

II.

Insbesondere legt die deutsche Delegation aufgrund ihrer eingehenden, dem Rat gegebenen Darlegungen Verwahrung gegen folgende Punkte ein:

1. Sie weist die Anschauung zurück, als gebe es in der Deutschen Evangelischen Kirche ein »autokratisches Kirchenregiment«. Es handelt sich vielmehr um eine Zusammenfassung in der kirchlichen Leitung und um Massnahmen der kirchlichen Ordnung.

2. Sie widerspricht der Meinung, als sei im Deutschen Reich die freie Verkündigung des Evangeliums in Wort und Schrift gefährdet und die christliche Erziehung der Jugend nicht gewährleistet. Sie bekennt vielmehr, dass die allgemeinen Verhältnisse im heutigen Deutschland der Verkündigung des Evangeliums viel mehr Möglichkeiten geben als zuvor.

3. Die deutsche Delegation lehnt die einseitige Heraushebung einer besonderen deutschen kirchlichen Gruppe und die Festlegung des Rates auf deren theologische Sondermeinung ab. Sie erblickt darin eine Stellungnahme zu innerdeutschen kirchlichen Verhältnissen, welche die Grenzen der Aufgabe des Oekumenischen Rates bedenklich überschreitet.

Liste des delegues

Nom:

Abernethy B.S.
Blackman E.C.
Blauenfeldt J.Miss
Bonhoeffer D.
Borghammer G.
Brandenburg W.
Brauer W.
Burlingham R.E.
Carter Keyna Miss
Chandi P.T.
Craske F.W.T.
Dudzus O.
Enterlein H.Frl.
Engberg E.Miss
Fabinyi E.
Forell Birger
Frik L.Frl.
Gerritsen Fie Frl.
Hoffer M.Frl.
Hurst N.H.
Josefson R.
Karding I.Frl.
Kilborn I.E.Mrs.
Kilborn T.H.H.
Klaveness B.
Kramm H.H.
Kühn R.
Lasserre J.
Mackay N.
Maechler W.
Martinesque J.
Matsuda R.
Møller S.A.
Nissen I.Miss
Parm Miss
Petersen S.
Pichal E.
Pichal N.Mme.
Rajaobelina P.
Ricoeur J.P.
Scharling C.J.
Skovgaard H.
Somos B.
Spock J.
Sturm Marcel
Synge E.Miss
Thyagaraju A.F.
Tillich E.
Toureille P.C.
Tweedie-Stodart Miss
Watson D.Miss
Winterhager J.
Zaunar L.
Zernoff N.
Ammundsen P.
Palansky
Felice Th. de
Toscoz M.Mlle.

left above and below:
Ecumenical Council for Practical Christianity: "Resolutions on the state of the church in Germany" (August 30, 1934), "Declaration of the German delegation."

center:
Ecumenical youth conference, August 22-29 in Fanö: Bonhoeffer's copy of the list of delegates.

endeavored to secure at least an official invitation to Fanö for representatives of the Confessing Church, and he was successful. On July 18, Karl Koch, the president of the Confessing Church, received from the bishop of Chichester the invitation for which they had hoped. Friedrich von Bodelschwingh was also invited by the president of the Council to come to Fanö, but the political situation in the aftermath of Röhm's murder and von Hindenburg's death made this impracticable. Bonhoeffer was disappointed.

On the very first day of its debates, the conference began to discuss the situation of the church in Germany. Five days later, on August 30, 1934, in dramatic circumstances, the "Resolutions on the situation of the church in Germany" were passed; in protest, the delegation from the German National Church issued a declaration denouncing this text. On the same day, Bonhoeffer and President Koch were elected "consultative and co-opted members" of the Council. Bishop Heckel protested against the election of President Koch.

Bonhoeffer himself regarded the "Resolutions on the situation of the church in Germany" as immeasurably more exciting than his own contributions to the conference as a lecturer and preacher. He had prepared the theses for his lecture on "The church and the world of the nations" at the beginning of August, a time of great turmoil: Italian troops marched up to the Austrian border, the disarmament negotiations broke down irreparably, war threatened to break out in Abyssinia. These were not the birth pangs of a new world! For Bonhoeffer, they confirmed the prophecy that Hitler meant war.

On the beach in Fanö, Bonhoeffer was asked by a Swedish participant: "What would you do if a war came, Pastor?" Bonhoeffer is said to have let the sand run through his fingers, then to have looked calmly at the questioner and said: "I pray that God will give me the strength then not to take up weapons."

On August 28, 1934, Bonhoeffer preached at morning worship. His text was Psalm 85:9, "Let me hear what God the Lord says, that he speaks peace to his people and to his saints, that they may not succumb to folly." His sermon bears the traces of those somber weeks, but its significance is far from limited to the days of Hitler.

How does peace come? Through a system of political treaties? Through the investment of international capital in the various countries, i.e., through the big banks, through money? Or perhaps through a multilateral peaceful armament intended to make peace secure? No, not through any of this – for the one simple reason that peace is confused here with security. The path of security is not the path to peace. For peace entails audacity, it is a very hazardous business and can never be made secure. Peace is the opposite of security. To demand security is to show that one lacks trust – and this distrust in turn gives birth to war.

Let us ask again: How does peace come? Who issues the summons to peace in such a way that the world hears it, indeed is compelled to hear it, so that all the peoples are compelled to rejoice in it? The individual Christian cannot do this. He can indeed raise his voice when everyone else is silent, and he can give his testimony, but the powers of the world can march over him word-

lessly. The individual church too can bear witness and suffer – would that it did indeed do so! – but it too is crushed by the power of hatred. Only the one great ecumenical council of the holy church of Christ from all the world can say it in such a way that the world will grind its teeth as it is compelled to hear the word of peace. And the peoples will then rejoice, because this church of Christ takes the weapons out of the hands of its sons in the name of Christ, and forbids them to engage in war, calling out the peace of Christ over the raging world.

From left: Dietrich Bonhoeffer, Jürgen Winterhager, Winfried Maechler (Fanö, 1934).

More than fifty persons took part in the youth conference under Bonhoeffer's direction, and they drew up two resolutions. The first led to vigorous debates. It proclaimed that God's commandments had priority over every claim made by the state, and was intended partly to offer an inherent justification for condemnations by the foreign press of events in Germany. Bonhoeffer strengthened this point by an addition to the text; the original version in his own handwriting has survived. The resolution was passed, but with the highest number of contrary votes, even among the German participants, most of whom were his own students.

The second resolution rejected support for any war. Here too, there were protests. Instead of "any war whatsoever," the formulation "aggressive war" was suggested. It was only after the discussion was interrupted for a period of meditation and prayer in common that the original formulation "any war whatsoever" was retained.

On the day of Bonhoeffer's sermon about peace in Fanö, his friend Jean Lasserre announced the resolutions of the youth conference in the full assembly of the World Alliance.

The church struggle, 1934–1935

On September 23, in the cathedral in Berlin, Ludwig Müller was installed as national bishop. This was followed by attempts to integrate the federal-state churches in southern Germany by force into the National Church, and Bishops Wurm and Meiser were placed under house arrest. This prompted the National Council of Brethren to convoke a National Confessing Synod to meet in Berlin-Dahlem on October 19-20, 1934.

The resolutions at Dahlem were unambiguous and unanimous: "The men who seize control of the church leadership on national and federal-state level have excluded themselves by their own actions from the Christian church." They went on to set up an emergency church leadership for the Confessing Church with a system of Councils of Brethren who formed a "Temporary church leadership of the German Protestant church" together with the leaderships of the "intact churches"; Bishop Marahrens was appointed president. The next step was to refuse obedience to the existing leadership of the National Church.

The decision for which Bonhoeffer had hoped was taken at Dahlem. Should they now wait to see whether the emergency church leadership would win acceptance by others and take on a stable form? Bonhoeffer took it for granted that the new system of leadership must be implemented without delay. Only this concrete implementation would give the Confessing synod and its organs of government the stability they needed to continue on their chosen path.

above:
Berlin cathedral, September 1934: national bishop Ludwig Müller is installed, without any ecumenical guests.

below:
Resolutions of the Dahlem Confessing Synod.

III.

1. Wir stellen fest: Die Verfassung der Deutschen Evangelischen Kirche ist zerschlagen. Ihre rechtmäßigen Organe bestehen nicht mehr. Die Männer, die sich der Kirchenleitung im Reich und in den Ländern bemächtigten, haben sich durch ihr Handeln von der christlichen Kirche geschieden.

2. Auf Grund des kirchlichen Notrechts der an Schrift und Bekenntnis gebundenen Kirchen, Gemeinden und Träger des geistlichen Amtes schafft die Bekenntnissynode der Deutschen Evangelischen Kirche neue Organe der Leitung. Sie beruft zur Leitung und Vertretung der Deutschen Evangelischen Kirche als eines Bundes bekenntnisbestimmter Kirchen den Bruderrat der Deutschen Evangelischen Kirche und aus seiner Mitte den Rat der Deutschen Evangelischen Kirche zur Führung der Geschäfte. Beide Organe sind den Bekenntnissen entsprechend zusammengesetzt und gegliedert.

3. Wir fordern die christlichen Gemeinden, ihre Pfarrer und Ältesten auf, von der bisherigen Reichskirchenregierung und ihren Behörden keine Weisungen entgegenzunehmen und sich von der Zusammenarbeit mit denen zurückzuziehen, die diesem Kirchenregiment weiterhin gehorsam sein wollen. Wir fordern sie auf, sich an die Anordnungen der Bekenntnissynode der Deutschen Evangelischen Kirche und der von ihr anerkannten Organe zu halten.

On November 5, 1934, the parish councils of almost all the German Protestant churches in England met in the German Christ Church in London under the chairmanship of Pastor Wehrhan. Dietrich Bonhoeffer informed them about the state of the church in Germany, and Pastor Rieger about the impact that the church struggle made in other countries. Forty-four parish council members from nine parishes declared "that they adhere with inner conviction to the position of the Confessing Church."

The members of the parish councils of St. Paul and Sydenham, assembled here, declare unanimously that they refuse to acknowledge the leadership of the National Church which is at present governed by National Bishop L. Müller. The parishes of St. Paul and Sydenham can no longer tolerate a church leadership whose goals and methods repudiate the most elementary principles of the Protestant faith. The members of the parish councils also affirm that the un-Protestant conduct of the National Church leadership in the course of the past eighteen months has gravely damaged the reputation of the German Reich in other countries. The parish council members declare that they are willing to acknowledge the National Church constitution, brought into being by a national law on July 15, 1933, as the legal basis for membership in the National Church, and that they continue to feel themselves united to a German Protestant church which would stand on this basis.

One week later, this resolution was communicated to the Confessing Synod in Bad Oeynhausen, with the request that Bonhoeffer and Pastor Schönberger be received for negotiations about joining the Synod.

above:
Resolution by Bonhoeffer's London parishes, January 4, 1935.

below:

Members of the National Council of Brethren and staff of the committee of the Temporary Church Leadership of the Confessing Church at a meeting in Bad Oeynhausen in January, 1935.
From the left: von Soden, Flor, Fiedler, von Arnim-Kröchlendorff, Sammetreuther, Koch, Asmussen, Kloppenburg, Müller-Dahlem, Link, Dürr, von Thadden-Trieglaff, Bosse, Beckmann.

Decision to return to Germany

Bonhoeffer had long wished to go to India to meet Mahatma Gandhi and share in his life. In the summer of 1934, Mira Bai (earlier known as Madeline Slade) came to England. She was the daughter of an English admiral and had taken part in Gandhi's work since 1925 as a disciple in his ashram. She had given away her personal property. Imperturbable like Gandhi, she too had done time in prison. Bonhoeffer read the newspaper reports about her and heard her speak. Bishop Bell sent a letter of recommendation to Gandhi, and Bonhoeffer hoped for an invitation to India.

Bonhoeffer's energies were completely taken up with parish work, aid to refugees, the church struggle, ecumenical contacts, and his plans for a voyage to India. But he could not forget the great pleasure he had always found in teaching theology and in writing, ever since he had begun his studies; and he felt that this was his vocation. When the national bishop shut down the Old Prussian seminaries for preachers in 1934 and demanded that students of theology produce proof of "Aryan" descent before they were permitted to take their examinations, the Confessing Church was forced to take theological education into its own hands. On July 14, 1934, Martin Niemöller closed the meeting of the Old Prussian Council of Brethren with the words: "Bonhoeffer can begin work as director of the seminary for preachers in Berlin-Brandenburg on January 1, 1935."

above:
Gandhi planting a tree in December 1931, in remembrance of his stay in London.

below:
Memorial tablet to Methodist missionaries in the entrance hall to Richmond College.

On September 11, 1934, Bonhoeffer wrote to Erwin Sutz: "I am struggling to take a decision whether I should return to Germany as the head of a preachers' seminary which is not yet opened – whether I should remain here – or whether I will go to India. I no longer believe in the university; indeed, I have never really believed in it, and this irritates the university world. The entire training of the new generation of theologians belongs today in ecclesiastical-monastic schools, in which pure doctrine, the Sermon on the Mount, and worship are taken seriously."

Before Bonhoeffer began his own attempt at "life in common," he visited Anglican seminaries and monasteries in England. He was greatly impressed by the tablet commemorating the Methodist missionaries in Richmond College: before each name was the year of entry, and after each name (often only a few years later), the year of the early death.

When Gandhi's invitation arrived in November, the events surrounding the secession of the London parishes from the National Church were blowing up to a storm. It was impossible for him to abandon his parishes and his colleagues now. With a heavy heart, Bonhoeffer gave up his plan to go to India.

November 1, 1934

Dear Friend,

I have received your letter. If you and your friend have enough money for the return journey and for your expenses here – let us say 100 rupees per person per month – you may come whenever you wish. The sooner the better, so that you may enjoy the cool weather we are having here. I have proposed 100 rupees per month as the absolute limit for someone who knows how to lead a simple life. It may in fact only cost you half that amount. Everything depends on how the climate here suits you.

With regard to your wish to share in my daily life, I would like to say to you that you can stay with me, unless I am in prison, and provided that I am staying in one place when you come. Otherwise, if I am traveling or in prison, you would have to be content with a stay in one or other of the institutions which are under my supervision. If you wish to live in one of these institutions which I have in mind, and are able to get by on the simplest vegetarian diet – which is all these institutions can offer you – you need not pay anything for food and lodging.

Yours sincerely
[Gandhi]

above:
The Methodist College in Richmond (1934).

below:
Mahatma Gandhi to Pastor Lic. D. Bonhoeffer.

Finkenwalde
(1935–37)

The Zingst farm

The first home of the Preachers' Seminary that the Council of Brethren in Berlin-Brandenburg had founded was Zingst, and this farm proved an ideal place of refuge. One hundred meters behind the dunes on the beach lies the half-timbered house, surrounded by its outbuildings with their low thatched roofs. The buildings covered the ground up towards the moor and the Barther Bodden. On clear days, one who stood on the dunes could see Hiddensee off the island of Rügen to the east. Whenever the May sun shone, they gathered in a hollow in the dunes for their discussions.

above:
Thatched outhouse on the Zingst farm.

below:
Candidates' study room; in the foreground A. Schönherr.

above:
On the Zingst farm.

below:
The Zingst farm near Barth on the Baltic Sea.

left page
Dietrich Bohoeffer,
August 1935.

Soon, they found a permanent home for the Seminary: the estate which had formerly belonged to the von Katte family in Finkenwalde, the first station on the important railway line eastward from Stettin. A badly built sport hall had been added to the main building, which had previously housed a private school. This had fallen victim to the National Socialist school policy.

Finkenwalde railway station.

Under the direction of the sculptor Wilhelm Gross, a persecuted "non-Aryan," the seminarians applied distemper, wood from crates, and untreated cotton to turn the sport hall into the chapel of the Finkenwalde seminary. On its end wall stood in gold letters the programmatic Greek word *hapax*, "once for all," from the Letter to the Hebrews. This is a concise summary of everything confessed by the "Theological Declaration of the Confessional Synod of Barmen" (a text basically composed by Karl Barth) in its first thesis, which was directed against the "German Christian" heresy concerning revelations in modern history.

On March 16, the Treaty of Versailles was breached with the passing of the "Law for the Build-up of the Army." When Hitler proclaimed on the Tempelhofer Field in Berlin on May 1, 1935, that Germany was once again a nation able to fight, most of the candidates in Finkenwalde welcomed this. A question posed by Bonhoeffer while the Führer's discourse was being broadcast on the radio provoked a heated discussion. Most of the brethren were quite unwilling to accept his claim that it was possible for Christians to refuse to take part in military service.

above:
Chapel of the seminary and of the Confessing Church parish in Finkenwalde.

right:
Law for the Build-up of the Army, March 16, 1935.

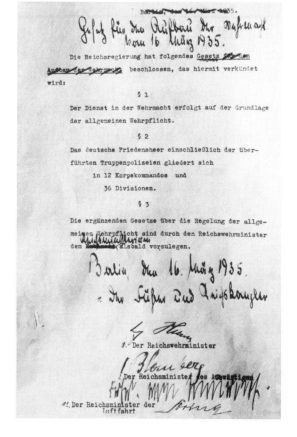

1. „Ich bin der Weg und die Wahrheit und das Leben; niemand kommt zum Vater denn durch mich." (Joh. 14, 6).

„Wahrlich, wahrlich ich sage euch: Wer nicht zur Tür hineingeht in den Schafstall, sondern steigt anderswo hinein, der ist ein Dieb und ein Mörder. Ich bin die Tür; so jemand durch mich eingeht, der wird selig werden." (Joh. 10, 1. 9).

Jesus Christus, wie er uns in der heiligen Schrift bezeugt wird, ist das eine Wort Gottes, das wir zu hören, dem wir im Leben und im Sterben zu vertrauen und zu gehorchen haben.

Wir verwerfen die falsche Lehre, als könne und müsse die Kirche als Quelle ihrer Verkündigung außer und neben diesem einen Worte Gottes auch noch andere Ereignisse und Mächte, Gestalten und Wahrheiten als Gottes Offenbarung anerkennen.

Bonhoeffer did not share the satisfaction felt by most members of the Confessing Church at the National Confessing Synod held in Augsburg from June 2 to 6, 1935. He held that the synod had incurred guilt, in that it had not managed to say anything clear about the freedom of the church and had kept silent both about the lies of the National Socialist Party program (§24: "Positive Christianity") and about the so-called Jewish question. Bonhoeffer had already been informed by his brother-in-law, Hans von Dohnanyi, about the answer the government intended to give this "question" in the "Nuremberg laws," which were then in preparation. Finally, the synod had said nothing about the military oath, which could not be accepted without reservation by Christians.

Karl Barth was willing to swear the oath required

above:
Bonhoeffer's private copy of the "Theological Declaration of Barmen" with a handwritten addition to the first thesis: "*one* source of revelation."

left:
The "Pädagogium Finkenwalde," a private school; from 1935, home to the "Preachers' Seminary of the Confessing Church of the Old Prussian Union."

Cover of the program of the Augsburg National Confessing Church Synod, June 2-6, 1935.

of government employees only with the additional clause: "so far as I can justify doing so as a Christian." The southern Germans did not want him to stay in Augsburg, and he left Germany in June 1935. The candidates in Finkenwalde made copies of his letter of farewell. Barth wrote that the Confessing Church "has not yet a heart for millions of those who suffer injustice. ... It has not yet found one word for the simplest questions of public honesty. When it speaks, it speaks only to promote its own self."

Encounter with the landed aristocracy in Pomerania

Thanks to the location of the preachers' seminary in Pomerania, Bonhoeffer became acquainted with a world that had been virtually a closed book to him before. There were very few connections between the academic circles in Grunewald at that time and the agrarian, political, and military environment of the landed aristocracy. In the great Pomeranian houses, Bonhoeffer now met families who remained his good friends until the end of his life.

Here he met for the first time Maria von Wedemeyer, who was later to become his fiancée. Her grandmother, Ruth von Kleist-Retzow, was very interested in theology and gave him a great deal of help in Finkenwalde. She came to his services with her grandchildren, some of whom were confirmed by Bonhoeffer – though not the twelve-year-old Maria, whom he thought too young. Years later, he met her once again in her grandmother's house.

These simple, straightforward encounters between Bonhoeffer and the Pomeranian aristocratic families were possible because both sides were willing to set their inherited privileges in politics and the church at risk, in order to meet the demands of the times. The new divisions in Germany cut clean through both the scholarly world of Grunewald and the landed aristocracy.

above:
Manor of the von Kleist-Retzow family in Kieckow.

center:
Pätzig, residence of the von Wedemeyer family.

below:
Wedding of Klaus von Bismarck and Ruth-Alice von Wedemeyer in Pätzig, 1939. The couples, from the left: Hans von Wedemeyer and Gertrud von Bismarck; Ruth and Hans-Werner von Wedemeyer; Ruth and Hans-Jürgen von Kleist-Retzow.

Discipleship and life in common

In Finkenwalde, Bonhoeffer took up a subject that had fascinated him for years: discipleship. His book with this title was published in 1937. Bonhoeffer identifies the point of reference of the Christian faith as the figure of Christ, who is present now: "The life of Jesus Christ has not yet come to an end on this earth. Christ continues to lead his life in the life of those who follow him."

"Discipleship" always has a social form for Bonhoeffer: it is realized as church, community, and fellowship. In Finkenwalde, therefore, he set up a "Brothers' house" in which those who were willing to take part led a "common life" in accordance with a number of rules: prayer and meditation, fraternal exhortation, free personal confession of sins, theological work in common, and the commitment to answer any emergency call from the church. It was possible to leave this house at any time. The brotherhood would decide whether to admit candidates.

... I believe that I would really attain inner clarity and genuine honesty only if I truly began to take the Sermon on the Mount seriously. This is the only source of the power that can one day explode all the magic and the racket until only a few charred remnants survive of all the fireworks. The restoration of the church will surely come from a kind of new monasticism. The only feature this will have in common with the old monasticism is the uncompromising character of a life led in accordance with the Sermon on the Mount, as disciples of Christ. I believe that the time has come to gather people for such a life ...

The question of the Christian life has surfaced anew among the young students of theology. It is no longer acceptable to respond to this with slogans such as "enthusiasm" or "an un-Lutheran attitude," for they regard this as a mere evasion. The answer to this question can be given, not in an abstract manner, but only by means of a concrete, sober life led in common and by reflection in common on the commandments. The vague sensation that something in the life of the parish clergy is not right will be helped to find the clarity it needs only through the practical attempt at obeying the commandments in a common exercise. The fact that the credibility of our preaching suffers thanks to our life – and thanks to the lack of clarity about what the Christian life is – obliges pastors to a fresh reflection and a fresh attempt in praxis ... In order to preach the Word of God in the present and future church struggles in such a way that it will be a summons to decision and to the discernment of spirits, in order to be ready for the ministry of preaching in every newly arising situation of need, we require a group of completely free pastors who are ready to go to work at every instant. They must be ready to go wherever their ministry is required, no matter what the external circumstances may be, renouncing all the financial and other privileges of the clerical state. Since they come from a brotherhood and continually return to it, they will find the home and the fellowship there that they need for their ministry. The goal is not a monastic separation from the world, but the innermost concentration in preparation for the external ministry.

above:
First course in Finkenwalde, on the last day of studies, October 15, 1935.
First row, from left: W. Danicke, H. Dufft, housekeeper Erna Struwe with her son, F. Onnasch, J. Goebel, R. Zenke. Second row: W. Schrader, K. Bojack, H. Voelz, R. Grunow, G. Beckmann, W. Maechler. Third row: E. Bethge, G. Hellmann, E. Kunert, H. Thiel, W. Rott. Upper row: H. Jehle, G. Vibrans, D. Bonhoeffer, H. Lekszas, W. Dell, J. Kanitz, A. Fr. Preuss, A. Schönherr.

center:
From a letter to his brother, Karl-Friedrich Bonhoeffer, January 14, 1935.

below:
To the Council of the Protestant Church of the Old Prussian Union, Berlin-Dahlem, concerning the foundation of a brotherhood house in the preachers' seminary at Finkenwalde, September 6, 1935.

Move to the Marienburger Allee

Since Dietrich's father was soon to retire, his parents planned to sell the big house in Wangenheimstraße in Grunewald. On October 1, 1935, Karl and Paula Bonhoeffer moved into a newly built house near the Heerstraße in Charlottenburg. Nr. 43 in the Marienburger Allee, a house surrounded by high pinetrees, was built to their own specifications. The attic room looking to the west now became Dietrich's. From his windows, he looked across to Nr. 42, which was built at the same time by Rüdiger and Ursula Schleicher; it was here that Dietrich was arrested in 1943, and his brother Klaus was arrested eighteen months later.

In the fall of 1936, Karl and Paula Bonhoeffer took their driving license, in order to be independent of a chauffeur once he retired from work. He noted in his diary for New Year's Eve: "We have both passed this examination – presumably the last we will ever take – with good results, even if not with excellent marks."

In 1937, the Charité celebrated the silver jubilee of Dietrich's father as director of the psychiatric clinic. Although he had retired, as the law required, on April 1, 1936, he was asked to continue in his post, and it was only in the summer of 1938 that he held his farewell lecture, surrounded by his colleagues. His three sons sat among the public on the benches in the auditorium. A great period at the clinic was now over. A new style arrived with Professor de Crinis, who belonged to the SS.

above:
The parents' house, flanked by the house of their daughter and son-in-law, Ursula and Robert Schleicher, Marienburger Allee 42 and 43. They moved in on October 1, 1935.

center:
The parents, Paula and Karl Bonhoeffer (photographs taken for their driving licenses).

below:
Farewell lecture of Karl Bonhoeffer, July 1938. From left E. Bethge, D. and K.-Fr. Bonhoeffer, to the right, Karl Bonhoeffer in conversation with his colleagues Stöckel and Sauerbruch; on the far right, von Eicken.

above:
The members of the church committees. From left: first row, Superintendent Zimmermann, Berlin (Prussia); retired General Superintendent D. Zoellner, Düsseldorf (national level); retired General Superintendent D. Eger, Naumburg (national level and Prussia); President Koopmann, Aurich (national level). Second row: Church Counselor Hanemann, Munich (national level); Pastor Kuessner, Kötzen (national level and Prus-sia); Pastor Wilm, Dolgelin/Mark (national level); federal-state bishop Diehl, Speyr (national level); Federal-State Church Counselor Dr. Mahrenholz, Hanover (national level); Superintendent Dr. Schmidt, Oberhausen (Prussia); cathedral preacher Martin, Magdeburg (Prussia); Consistorial Counselor Kaminski, Königsberg (Prussia).

center right:
National Church Minister Hanns Kerrl.

below:
Fourth resolution of the Steglitz Synod.

Vierter Beschluß:

Die derzeitige Art der öffentlichen Behandlung der Judenfrage ist weiterhin verbunden mit einer Bestreitung des Evangeliums und der christlichen Kirche.

Angesichts der dadurch unseren Gemeinden drohenden Verwirrung wolle der Reichsbruderrat baldigst für eine nach Schrift und Bekenntnis richtungweisende Antwort auf die einzelnen damit gestellten Fragen Sorge tragen.

"Pacification" of the church?

In the summer of 1935, Hitler set up a Church Ministry headed by Hanns Kerrl. General Superintendent Zoellner was commissioned to "pacify" the church by means of so-called church committees, which were to be composed of men from the Confessing Church, the German Christians, and those who were neutral. Zoellner's invitation to collaboration contained a solemn proclamation: "We approve of the National Socialist formation of a people on the basis of race, blood, and soil." Ought one to participate? A deep fissure opened up in the ranks of the Confessing Church.

In this situation, the Old Prussian Confessing Synod met in Berlin-Steglitz from September 23 to 26, 1935, and discussed urgent problems of financial responsibility within the church and of spiritual leadership by the Councils of Brethren. A ministerial director of Kerrl's ministry was present — and they spoke against him! But there was another, very different element in the background to this synod: on September 15, Hitler had promulgated the "Nuremberg Laws," viz., the "law for the protection of blood," the prohibition of so-called mixed marriages, and the "Law concerning National Citizenship" which deprived the Jews of full political rights. On the first morning, the preachers' seminary in Finkenwalde attended the synod in Steglitz as a pressure group in the gallery. The synod laboriously reached agreement on a defense of the mission to the Jews and baptism of Jews — a daring thing to do by that date. Ought it not to have "opened its mouth for those who have no voice," ten days after the "Nuremberg Laws" had been made public? It did not do so. It delegated to the National Council of Brethren the task of discussing the general problems related to the Jews.

On December 2, the "Fifth Ordinance for the Implementation of the Law for the Consolidation of the Protestant Church" was promulgated. It forbade all "ordinances concerning church government and church offices by ecclesiastic associations or groups." This meant that it was now illegal to conduct a preachers' seminary in the name of the Brotherhood Councils. On the evening of December 2, Bonhoeffer called all the candidates together and told them that, in view of the new situation, they were free to leave. All remained.

Journey to Sweden, 1936

To mark Bonhoeffer's thirtieth birthday, the students in his second course expressed the wish to go on a study trip to Sweden. Thanks to Bonhoeffer's ecumenical contacts, an invitation was issued by Nils Karlström in the name of the Ecumenical Committee of the Swedish Church:

February 22, 1936

To the Director of the preachers' seminary of the Confessing Church at Finkenwalde:

It is my honor to invite the preachers' seminary herewith to a study trip to Sweden from March 1 to 10, so that they may become better acquainted with church life in Sweden in Lund, Uppsala, Sigtuna, and Stockholm. It would be a pleasure for us to provide food and lodging for the brethren of the seminary during this period.

In the hope that you will be able to accept this invitation, I remain,

Yours devotedly,

Signed: Nils Karlström
Secretary of the Swedish Ecumenical Committee

above:
Second course in Finkenwalde, with members of the first course who belonged to the brotherhood house. First row, from left: Schemann, Rose, Onnasch, Struwe, Koch, Büchsel, E. Müller, Schaaf. Second row: Lekszas, Pompe, Büsing, Schlegel, Rütenik, Berg. Third row: Bonhoeffer, Harhausen, K.F. Müller, Mrs. Struwe, Rhode, Trentepohl, Rott. Fourth row: Schönherr, Schlagowsky, Lohmann, von der Marwitz, Bethge.

below:
Bishop D. Heckel's letter to the National Church Committee in Berlin, March 7, 1936.

Berlin-Charlettenburg 2, den 7.März 1936

An

den Landeskirchenausschuss

h i e r

Von dem ökumenischen Ausschuss der schwedischen Kirche ist der Privatdozent Pfarrer Lic. Bonhoeffer, Leiter eines Bekenntnis-Seminars in Finkenwalde bei Stettin, mit dem Bekenntnis-Seminar zu einem Gastaufenthalt nach Schweden eingeladen worden. Die aussenpolitische Seite dieses Aktes wird von den zuständigen Stellen behandelt. Ich möchte aber nicht versäumen, den Landeskirchenausschuss darauf aufmerksam gemacht zu haben, dass Lic. Bonhoeffer durch diese Begebenheit sehr in das Licht der Oeffentlichkeit gerückt ist. Da der Vorwurf gegen ihn erhoben werden kann, dass er Pazifist und Staatsfeind ist, dürfte es angebracht sein, dass der Landeskirchenausschuss sich deutlich distanziert und Massnahmen ergreift, dass nicht länger deutsche Theologen von ihm erzogen werden.

gez. D. Heckel.

Wfan 16.5.36.

Sehr verehrter Herr Erzbischof !

Für Euer Gnaden freundliches Schreiben vom 13.März 1936 darf ich meinen aufrichtigen Dank sagen. Ich habe daraus ersehen, dass die Einladung an Herrn Lic. Bonhoeffer durchaus nicht offiziell, sondern persönlich und freundschaftlich gemeint war. Dass meine Sorge, solche freundschaftlich gemeinten Einladungen möchten nachher kirchenpolitisch missdeutet werden nicht unbegründet war, zeigt die Tatsache, dass die Teilnehmer der Studienreise selber in gedruckten Berichten der "Bekennenden Kirche" neuerdings auch in der "Jungen Kirche" mit Nachdruck betont haben, dass es sich bei ihrer Reise um eine offizielle Einladung, offizielle Empfänge etc. gehandelt habe. Ich bitte Sie deshalb verstehen zu wollen, dass ich meinen Brief aus der Verantwortung für die Leitung der Deutschen Kirche schreiben musste. Wir sind mit Ihnen sehr froh über jeden freundschaftlichen und brüderlichen Austausch mit den Brüdern anderer lutherischer Kirchen und möchten diesen Austausch in keiner Weise hemmen. Ich stimme dabei den letzten Sätzen Ihres Briefes völlig zu. Aber ich trage vor Gott die Verantwortung dafür, dass die grosse Aufgabe, unserem Volk ein einheitliche und geschlossene reformatorische Kirche zu erhalten, nicht erschwert wird. Aus dieser nicht unbegründeten Sorge

Sorge war mein Brief geschrieben. Umso dankbarer war ich für Ihre umgehende Antwort.

In aufrichtiger Verehrung bin ich Euer Gnaden ganz ergebener

Zoellner

above left:
March 3, 1936: arrival in Stockholm.

above right:
Archbishop D. Erling Eidem.

left:
D. Wilhelm Zoellner to Archbishop Eidem.

The program included visits to Lund, Uppsala, and Sigtuna. On March 4, D. Erling Eidem, archbishop of Uppsala, held a reception for the Finkenwalde seminary, and the important Swedish newspapers carried reports on their front pages. In Germany, the Church Foreign Office regarded this as an evasion of its own attempts to exercise strict control over German ecumenical relationships, and grievances that had festered since 1933 now led to harsh reactions: Bishop D. Heckel accused Bonhoeffer of being "a pacifist and an enemy of the state," and recommended that measures be taken "to prevent German theologians from being educated by him in future."

On the initiative of the Church Foreign Office, the president of the National Church Committee got in touch with Archbishop Eidem: when the Swedish church issued an official invitation, was it siding with the Confessing Church and against the "responsible leadership of the German Protestant Church"? Eidem's dilemma was exploited by Zoellner: "This showed me that the invitation to Mr. Bonhoeffer was certainly not official, but was meant in a private and friendly context."

No salvation outside the Confessing Church?

Was it possible in the long term for the Confessing Church to cooperate with the church committees which had been appointed by the National Church Ministry? The National Synod of the Confessing Church, held at Oeynhausen in February, 1936, avoided giving a clear answer. In June 1936, Dietrich Bonhoeffer published an essay "On the Question of Church Membership" in the periodical *Evangelical Theology*. One sentence became immediately famous in church circles in Germany: "Whoever knowingly separates from the Confessing Church in Germany is separating from salvation." This article was discussed on all levels in the church; questions were put and measures proposed by those who saw it as "legalism," "enthusiasm," "erroneous teaching," and "heresy." Bonhoeffer replied: "If the Barmen Declaration is a true confession of faith in the Lord Jesus, which is brought about by the Holy Spirit, then it is a text which builds up the church and also splits the church. Otherwise, it is only the expression of the opinion of a few theologians, and is not binding – and in that case, the Confessing Church has been pursuing a false path since then, with terrible consequences."

On August 5, 1936, Bonhoeffer was stripped of his authorization to teach as Privatdozent at the University of Berlin. The prohibitions issued by the church's institutes of higher studies, and the increasing Nazification of the universities, compelled the Confessing Church to make provisions for those who studied at the theological faculties. In the summer of 1936, Bonhoeffer was in Greifswald almost every week, holding "substitute lectures." Countess Behr made her manor available for this purpose. Albrecht Schöner founded a house of residence in the same style as Finkenwalde.

above:
On the Behrenhoff estate, May 1936: E. Bethge lecturing.

center:
Listeners on the Behrenhoff estate (fourth from left, Countess Mechthild Behr).

below:
Title page of the periodical *Evangelische Theologie*, June 1935, and an excerpt from the article mentioned here.

Evangelische Theologie

Extra ecclesiam nulla salus. Die Frage nach der Kirchengemeinschaft ist die Frage nach der Heilsgemeinschaft. Die Grenzen der Kirche sind die Grenzen des Heils. Wer sich wissentlich von der Bekennenden Kirche in Deutschland trennt, trennt sich vom Heil. Das ist die Erkenntnis, die sich der wahren Kirche von jeher aufgezwungen hat. Das ist ihr demütiges Bekenntnis. Wer die Frage nach der Bekenntniskirche von der Frage nach seinem Seelenheil trennt, begreift nicht, daß der Kampf der Bekennenden Kirche der Kampf um sein Seelenheil ist.

Der Wortlaut der Protestschrift der Deutschen Evangelischen Kirche an Reichskanzler Hitler

Wir veröffentlichen im folgenden die bedeutsame Denkschrift der Vorläufigen Leitung der Deutschen Evangelischen Kirche, die — wie unsere Leser bereits wissen — kürzlich dem Reichskanzler Hitler durch Staatssekretär Meißner zugeleitet worden ist, im vollen Wortlaut, da sie die derzeitige Lage der Evangelischen Kirche in Deutschland und das Verhältnis des evangelischen Christentums zum Nationalsozialismus in klarer und umfassender Form zur Darstellung bringt. Die Sperrungen im Text stammen von uns. Die Redaktion.

„Die Deutsche Evangelische Kirche, vertreten durch die geistlichen Mitglieder ihrer Vorläufigen Leitung und den dieser zur Seite stehenden Rat, entbietet dem Führer und Reichskanzler ehrerbietigen Gruß.

Die Deutsche Evangelische Kirche ist mit dem Führer und seinen Ratgebern eng verbunden durch die Fürbitte, die sie öffentlich wie in der Stille für Volk, Staat und Regierung übt. Darum hat die Vorläufige Leitung der Deutschen Evangelischen Kirche in Verbindung mit dem Rat der Deutschen Evangelischen Kirche es auf sich nehmen dürfen, die Sorgen und Befürchtungen, die viele Christen in Gemeinden, Bruderräten und Kirchenleitungen im Blick auf die Zukunft des evangelischen Glaubens und der evangelischen Kirche in Deutschland bewegen und die sie lange und ernstlich durchdacht hat, in dem vorliegenden Schreiben zum Ausdruck zu bringen.

Sie übergibt dieses Schreiben im Gehorsam gegen ihren göttlichen Auftrag, vor jedermann — auch vor den Herren und Gebietern der Völker — ungescheut Sein Wort zu sagen und Sein Gebot zu bezeugen. Sie vertraut darauf, daß Gott ihr selbst die Weisheit schenkt, ihren Auftrag so klar und eindeutig auszuführen, daß dabei ihre Sorge um das christliche Gewissen und ihre Liebe zum deutschen Volk in gleicher Weise unmißverständlich erkennbar werden.

Wir wissen uns jedenfalls bei unseren Darlegungen, wie unsere Amtsvorgänger in ihrem leider ohne spürbare Wirkung gebliebenen Schreiben vom 11. April 1935 (in Anmerkung beigefügt), nur von der einen Pflicht getrieben, den leidenden, verwirrten und gefährdeten Gliedern der evangelischen Kirche durch ihr Wort und ihre Fürsprache zu helfen. Es liegt uns alles daran, daß die Reichsregierung aus ihren Ausführungen diese aus der Sorge um die der Kirche anvertrauten Seelen sprechende Stimme klar und deutlich vernehme.

Der Herr der Kirche sagt: „Was hülfe es dem Menschen, so er die ganze Welt gewönne und nähme doch Schaden an seiner Seele? Oder was kann der Mensch geben, damit er seine Seele wieder löse?" Dieses Wort zeigt die Größe und den Ernst des Dienstes, zu dem die Kirche von Gott gerufen ist. Es erinnert zugleich an die Grenzen, die allen irdischen Mächten und ihrem Streben gesteckt sind. Es weist endlich auf die Gefahr hin, der immer wieder unzählige Menschen, darunter auch Glieder der Kirche, zu erliegen drohen.

1. Gefahr der Entchristlichung.

Die Vorläufige Leitung weiß es zu würdigen, was es im Jahre 1933 und späterhin bedeutet hat, daß die Träger der nationalsozialistischen Revolution nachdrücklich erklären konnten: „Wir haben mit unserem Sieg über den Bolschewismus zugleich den Feind überwunden, der auch das Christentum und die christlichen Kirchen bekämpfte und zu zerstören drohte."

Wir erleben aber, daß der Kampf gegen die christliche Kirche, wie nie seit 1918, im Deutschen Volke wirksam und lebendig ist.

Keine Macht der Welt, wie sie auch heiße, vermag die Kirche Gottes gegen Seinen Willen zu zerstören oder zu schützen; das ist Gottes Sache. Die Kirche aber hat sich der angefochtenen Gewissen ihrer Glieder anzunehmen.

Durch die Not und Verwirrung des heutigen Glaubenskampfes werden viele getaufte Christen mit zeitlichem und ewigem Unheil bedroht. Wenn sogar hohe Stellen in Staat und Partei den Christenglauben öffentlich angreifen (Anm. u. a. Rede Leys), dann werden der Kirche und ihrer Botschaft an sich schon entfremdete Kirchenglieder dadurch immer mehr in ihrem Unglauben verstrickt, Wankende und Unsichere vollends unsicher gemacht und zum Abfall getrieben. Ja, es besteht ernstliche Gefahr, daß die evangelische Jugend sich hindern läßt, zu dem zu kommen, der der alleinige Heiland auch deutscher Knaben und Mädchen ist. Dieser Gefährdung der Glieder der Kirche muß eine verantwortungsbewußte Kirchenleitung wehren.

Zu solcher Abwehr gehört die klare Frage an den Führer und Reichskanzler, ob der Versuch, das deutsche Volk zu entchristlichen, durch verantwortlicher Staatsmänner oder auch nur durch Zulassen und Gewährenlassen zum offiziellen Kurs der Regierung werden soll.

2. „Positives Christentum."

Wir vertrauen, daß die Reichsregierung, um die Zuspitzung des Glaubenskampfes in Deutschland zu vermelden, das Wort der evangelischen Kirche hören wird. Als die N.S.D.A.P. in ihrem Programm erklärte, daß sie auf dem Boden eines „positiven Christentums" stehe, hat die gesamte kirchliche Bevölkerung das dahin verstehen müssen und auch verstehen sollen, daß im Dritten Reich der christliche Glaube gemäß den Bekenntnissen und der Predigt der Kirche Freiheit und Schutz, ja Hilfe und Förderung erfahren sollte.

Später aber ist es dahin gekommen, daß maßgebende Persönlichkeiten des Staates und der Partei das Wort „positives Christentum" willkürlich auslegten haben.

Bald gab der Herr Reichsminister für Propaganda und Volksaufklärung als positives Christentum aus, was lediglich humanitäre Leistung ist, und verband mit dieser Auslegung unter Umständen einen Angriff auf die christlichen Kirchen unter ihrer angeblich mangelhaften Leistungen auf dem Gebiet der christlichen Liebestätigkeit, das ihnen doch der Staat selbst seit 1933 durch seine Verbote wesentlich eingeengt hatte (Anm. Reden von Goebbels zum Winterhilfswerk u. a.): „Wären die Kirchen von wahrem christlichen Geist beseelt, dann hätten sie es niemals dem Staat überlassen, in diesem Winter den Armen über Hunger und Frost hinwegzuhelfen.. Ich glaube, Christus selbst würde in unserem Tun mehr von seiner Lehre entdecken als in diesen theologischen Haarspaltereien... Das Volk würde vielleicht eher verstehen, wenn die Kirche sich mit dem wahren Christentum beschäftigte..."); bald verkündete der Herr Reichsleitungsleiter Rosenberg keine Mystik des Blutes als positives Christentum, und Parteistellen diffamierten nach keinem Vorbild das bekenntnismäßig- und offenbarungsgläubige Christentum als negativ (Anm. Rosenberg. „Wir erkennen heute, daß die zentralen Höchstwerte der römischen und der protestantischen Kirche als negatives Christentum unserer Seele nicht entsprechen, daß sie den organischen Kräften der nordisch-rassisch bestimmten Völker im Wege stehen, ihnen Platz zu machen haben, sich neu im Sinne eines germanischen Christentums umwerten lassen müssen". Schreiben der

"Basler Nachrichten," July 23, 1936: text of the "Memorandum to Hitler" (excerpt).

Memorandum to Hitler

In the spring of 1936, the Temporary Leadership of the Confessing Church drew up a "Memorandum to Hitler." Franz Hildebrandt was a member of one of the preparatory working parties, and he consulted with Bonhoeffer. The Memorandum mentions antisemitism and hatred of the Jews, it speaks of the concentration camps, and does not mince words about the "measures taken by the Gestapo, which no judge is allowed to examine retrospectively." Now at last the Confessing Church raised its voice against unsettling developments in areas which did not directly concern church life. On July 23, 1936, six weeks after the Memorandum was handed over in the National Chancellery, it was published word for word in the "Basler Nachrichten." What had happened? Since Hitler had not replied, and the Temporary Leadership likewise did nothing, two of Bonhoeffer's students — Werner Koch and Ernst Tillich — decided to give this Memorandum the importance it deserved by publishing it abroad. Some time after this, both were arrested. On February 19, 1937, one of the authors, Friedrich Weißler, the baptized son of Jewish parents, died under torture by the SS in the concentration camp at Sachsenhausen.

Friedrich Weißler

The Finkenwalde mission

Was the Confessing Church wasting its energies on theological debates and legal wrangles? The German Christians were engaging in "missions among the people." National Bishop Ludwig Müller "Germanized" the Sermon on the Mount, so that the beatitude pronounced on the "meek" now became: "Blessed is the one who is always loyal to his comrades. He will get by in the world." For Bonhoeffer, the church struggle was inseparable from evangelization, and the seminarians went into the countryside for missionary work among the populace. Until Finkenwalde closed its doors, 36 parishes in Pomerania, the province of Saxony, and Brandenburg were visited by groups of four students.

left above:
Bonhoeffer with seminarians on the Baltic Sea, summer 1936.

left below:
Dietrich Bonhoeffer and Hans Asmussen on a brief missionary camp in Stecklenburg (province of Saxony).

below:
"German words of God": Bonhoeffer's manuscript commentaries on the "Germanization" of the Sermon on the Mount by National Bishop Ludwig Müller.

above:
Third course in Finkenwalde, last day of studies, August 16, 1936.

First row from left: G. Wichmann, R. Kühn, O. Lerche, H. Rabius, J. Lent, A. Richter, F. Onnasch. Second row: G. Seydel, K. Block, G. Wetzel, E. Schumacher, G. Riemer, G. Christ, K.F. Müller. Third row: H. Thurmann, R. Meinhof, A. Tetsch, G. Grosch, W. Marzahn, T. Maass, H. Lekszas. Fourth row: W. Rott, H. Matiwe, D. Bonhoeffer, M. Müller, W. Reimers, W.D. Zimmermann, H.O. Schumann.

Der ewige Christus spricht:

Wohl dem, der in kindlicher Einfalt Gott vertraut. Er hat Gemeinschaft mit Gott.

Wohl dem, der sein Leid mannhaft trägt. Er wird die Kraft finden, nie mutlos zu verzweifeln.

Wohl dem, der allzeit gute Kameradschaft hält. Er wird in der Welt zurecht kommen.

Wohl dem, der danach hungert und dürstet, mit Gott ins Reine zu kommen. Er wird Gottes Frieden finden.

Wohl dem, der barmherzig ist. Er wird Gottes Barmherzigkeit erfahren.

Wohl dem, der reines Herzens ist. Er hat Gemeinschaft mit Gott.

Wohl denen, die mit ihren Volksgenossen Frieden halten; sie tun Gottes Willen.

Wohl denen, die ehrlich und treu leben und arbeiten, die aber trotzdem verfolgt und verlästert werden — sie behalten Gemeinschaft mit Gott.

Wohl euch, wenn ihr um Gott und um eurer Treue zu ihm geschmäht und verfolgt werdet; oder wenn die Menschen fälschlich Böses und Niederträchtiges von euch reden. Seid fröhlich und unverzagt, so hat es die gottfremde Welt immer getrieben, so wurden auch schon eure eigenen frommen Väter verfolgt.

Ecumenical conference at Chamby

Three German delegations took part in the negotiations at the ecumenical conference at Chamby that prepared for the World Conference of Churches in Oxford: that of the Confessing Church (K. Koch, O. Dibelius, H. Böhm, D. Bonhoeffer), that of the Lutheran Council (H. Lilje), and that of the National Church Committee (W. Zoellner, F. Brunstäd) together with H. Wahl and T. Heckel. The negotiations which Bishop Bell conducted separately with each group suggested that it would be possible to have one single German delegation to Oxford, but there was no further discussion, nor was any resolution passed on the Jewish question. After the conference, Bonhoeffer had a short holiday in Italy. In the course of his journey home, he visited Erwin Sutz in Wiesendangen.

above:
Dietrich Bonhoeffer and Eberhard Bethge setting off for Chamby, August 18, 1936.

center:
Conference at Chamby, August 21-25, 1936. From left: President Koch, General Superintendent Zoellner, Bishop Bell, General Superintendent Dibelius.

below:
Dietrich Bonhoeffer with Eberhard Bethge, visiting Erwin Sutz in Wiesendangen near Zurich.

Prohibitions, arrests, and the end of Finkenwalde

The Church Ministry employed ordinances, prohibitions, and arrests as its instruments to destroy the church of the Brotherhood Councils. On June 23, 1937, the Gestapo forced their way into the meeting of the National Brotherhood Council in the Friedrich Werder Church in Berlin and arrested the members.

On the morning of July 1, Dietrich Bonhoeffer and Eberhard Bethge went to Dahlem for consultations with Martin Niemöller and Franz Hildebrandt in Cecilienstraße 61. Only a few minutes before their arrival, Niemöller was taken away – to become the "personal prisoner" of Hitler. After discussing the situation with Mrs. Niemöller and Eugen Rose (who was also present), the group saw the unmistakable convoy of black Mercedes limousines driving up the door. They were put under house arrest by the Gestapo and were thus involuntary witnesses to the search of Niemöller's study, which took eight hours. Two days later, Bishop Bell, who had been informed by Pastor Rose, wrote in the *London Times*: "This is a critical hour. It is not only a question of the fate of one German pastor. It is a question of the attitude of the German state to Christianity."

In the following months, a number of former students at Finkenwalde were also arrested. By Christmas of 1937, 27 of them had been in prison. With the help of the Bonhoeffer family, Franz Hildebrandt, who had already been imprisoned, was able to emigrate to England.

right page:

above:
Fifth and last course in Finkenwalde, last day of studies, September 8, 1937. Sitting, from left: K. Vosberg, W. Schmidt, Wolfgang Krause, E. Veckenstedt, Mrs. Struwe, F. Onnasch, Bonhoeffer, K. Kückes, G. Kuhrmann, G. Kleinschmidt. Center: O. Janikowski, H. Thurmann, H. Morlinghaus, A. Schröder, W. Brandenburg, H. Krüger, W. Schwichtenberg, H. Gadow, Winfried Krause, R. Hensel, R. Wapler, H. Liedtke, Bethge, H. Lekszas, G. Rohr, J. Taube. Upper row: K. Minnich, O. Dudzus, K.H. Corbach, P. Wälde, O. Kistner

below:
Official prohibition of the commissions of the Confessing Church which had exercised control of lecturers, students, and examinations.

above:
Martin Niemöller, ca. 1946.

below:
Fourth course in Finkenwalde, last day of studies, March 14, 1937. (Third row, from left: F. Schroeter, E. Klapproth, W. Rott, G. Ebeling, R. Schade, G. Krause.)

On August 29, 1937, on the instructions of the National Head of the SS and the head of the German police, the "substitute academic colleges set up by the so-called Confessing Church" were closed down.

While Bonhoeffer was on a family visit in Göttingen, he received an unexpected phone call from Stettin: the Gestapo had turned up in Finkenwalde. Fritz Onnasch and the housekeeper, Mrs. Struwe, were forced to accept the command to close the house and had to leave when the officers sealed the doors. Would it be possible to continue the work in another form? Would it be possible to evade the prohibition for a time? One possible refuge was in rural Pomerania.

"Collective vicariates"
(1938–39)

The form of theological education and life in common which had been tried out in Finkenwalde was able to continue for almost two and a half years, though of course under more primitive conditions. It was reduced to a small circle who were disguised as "collective vicariates."

In rural Pomerania, two neighboring superintendents were willing to appoint the seminarians officially as substitute teachers in parishes which lay close to each other, and to find a place for them to live in common. Friedrich Onnasch, the father of the inspector of studies in Finkenwalde, had himself been suspended temporarily from the ministry in 1934 because he was a member of the Confessing Church. He opened the doors of his spacious parish house in Köslin to one group.

In Schlawe, Eduard Block found a position for Bonhoeffer as assistant preacher; Dietrich gave the superintendent's house in the Koppelstraße as his residence when he registered with the police. Seventeen kilometers to the east of Schlawe, he and the other group moved into the crooked parish house of Gross-Schlönwitz. The tiny village served by this parish lies a few kilometers to the south of Highway nr. 2 from Köslin to Stolp. Here, the group could exist only thanks to the use of automobiles. Accordingly, the first step in their work was the purchase of a second car and a motorcycle – something unheard-of at that date.

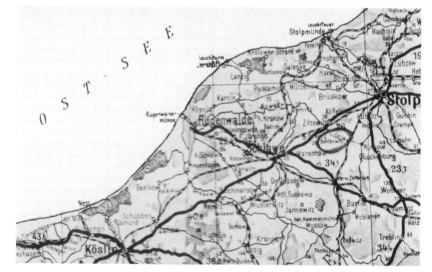

above left:
Superintendent Eduard Block and his wife.

above right:
Friedrich Onnasch.

center:
Section of a map of Köslin, Schlawe, and Stolp in Pomerania.

below:
Parish house in Groß-Schlönwitz, façade.

above:
February 7, 1938, setting out for the Baltic Sea.

below:
The "collective vicariate" from Groß-Schlönwitz on the Baltic Sea beach (second from left: Dietrich Bonhoeffer, beside him Heinz Fleischhack, far right Eberhard Bethge).

Training theologians illegally

On January 11, 1938, those responsible for theological training and the directors of the brotherhoods of substitute clergy in the Old Prussian Confessing Church in the parish house in Dahlem were put in prison. Dietrich Bonhoeffer was forbidden to enter the city of Berlin. His father succeeded in having this prohibition toned down, so that it applied only to matters of work; Dietrich was thus able to continue visiting his family in Berlin.

1938 was the year of the greatest weakness of the Confessing Church. On April 20, the leadership of the German Protestant church ordered all pastors in active ministry to take an oath of allegiance to the Führer: "I swear that I will be loyal and obedient to the Führer of the German nation and people, Adolf Hitler, that I will observe the laws and carry out the duties of my position conscientiously, so help me God" – "Anyone who refuses to swear this oath is to be dismissed from office." Since Bonhoeffer was no longer included in the consistory's lists of pastors, this decree about the oath did not affect him; nor did it affect those who were working illegally. In July, the Old Prussian Confessing Church synod allowed pastors to take the oath. Bonhoeffer saw this event as decisive: "Will the Confessing Church be willing to confess publicly its guilt and division?"

Groß-Schlönwitz, summer 1938.

Eingabe an die Geheime Staatspolizei.

Pastor Lic. Dietrich Bonhoeffer
Schlawe/Pom.   Koppelstr. 9

Mitte Januar 1938[1] wurde ich zu einer Besprechung kirchlicher Fragen nach Berlin eingeladen. Da ich ohnedies aus persönlichen Gründen in diesen Tagen zu meinem Vater nach Berlin fahren musste, sagte ich zu. Ich fand im Dahlemer Gemeindehaus, wo die Sitzung stattfinden sollte, einen Kreis von etwa 30 führenden Bekenntnispfarrern aus der ganzen Altpreuss. Union vor. Es sollte unter dem Vorsitz von Herrn Pf. Lic. Niesel über einige wichtige kirchliche Fragen gesprochen werden, besonders über die Möglichkeit der Unterstellung der Bekenntniskare und -Hilfsprediger unter die Konsistorien. Bereits nach einer halben Stunde erschienen Beamte der Geheimen Staatspolizei, brachten uns alle in grossen Polizeiwagen auf den Alexanderplatz; wir wurden vernommen; die nicht in Berlin und Brandenburg ansässigen Pfarrer wurden aus Berlin und Brandenburg ausgewiesen, die andern erhielten Ausreiseverbot aus Berlin und Brandenburg. Ein Grund für diese Massnahme wurde nicht angegeben. Die Sitzung war weder verboten noch, wie der Ort deutlich macht, besonders geheim gehalten, noch konnte ihr Gegenstand den Grund für besondere Massnahmen bieten. Wir haben nachträglich erfahren, dass man bei unserer Zusammenkunft irrtümlicherweise einen theologischen Vorlesungskurs für Studenten der Bekennenden Kirche vermutete und überrascht gewesen sei, keinen einzigen Studenten vorzufinden. Ich bin seitdem aus Berlin und Brandenburg ausgewiesen, wenngleich mir durch meinen Vater, Geheimrat Prof. K. Bonhoeffer, eine Aufenthaltserlaubnis für persönliche Besuche in Berlin bei der Geheimen Staatspolizei erwirkt worden ist. Jedoch bin ich nicht in der Lage, in meiner grossen in Berlin wohnenden Familie und in meinem Bekanntenkreis irgendwelche kirchlichen Handlungen vorzunehmen. Ausserdem belastet mich natürlich die mir nach wie vor unverständliche staatspolizeiliche Massnahme, die mich meinem Empfinden nach nur ganz zufällig getroffen hat und deren Ausmass mir in keinem Verhältnis zu ihrem Anlass zu stehen scheint.

Dietrich Bonhoeffer/

[1] Sitzung der Ausbildungsleiter u. Referenten der Bek. Kirche der APU am 11. Januar 1938, 9.30 vorm.

left page:

above:
Petition to the Gestapo,
January 1938.

below:
On a brief visit in Marienburger
Allee in Berlin. From left: Paula
Bonhoeffer, Hans Walter,
Dorothee and Christine Schlei-
cher, Dietrich Bonhoeffer.

right page:

above:
Summer 1938: Eberhard Bethge
and Dietrich Bonhoeffer, in the
parish house, Gross-Schlönwitz.

below:
July 10, 1938: Tea in the parish
house, Groß-Schlönwitz. From
left: H. Fleischhack, H. Bluhm,
D. Bonhoeffer, E. Bethge,
G. Lehne, H. Schröder, E. Engler.

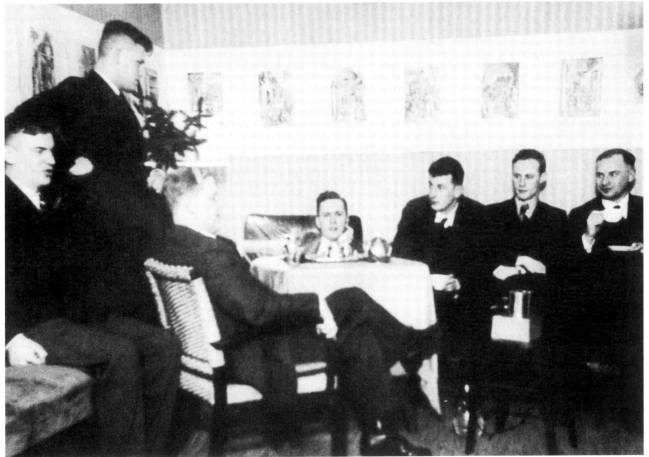

The risk of war; his twin sister emigrates

In the first year of the dictatorship, no one in the family had been able to imagine such a definitive parting. In the summer of 1938, the mobilization in connection with the Sudetenland crisis prompted the fear that the German borders would be closed. On September 9, Dietrich Bonhoeffer accompanied his twin sister, with her husband and their children, on part of their journey into exile. Before midnight, the Leibholz family crossed the border near Basle. In the fall, Bonhoeffer wrote *Discipleship* in their empty house. His experiences in Finkenwalde were uppermost in his mind at that time.

At the end of September 1938, the Temporary Leadership of the Confessing Church issued a liturgical form of service. An unusually courageous confession of guilt on the part of the German people was used, exhorting the parishes to pray that the imminent danger of war might come to nothing. The SS newspaper *The Black Corps* replied under the heading: "The security of the people," that "the extermination of these criminals is an obligation of the state."

Gemeinsames Leben (*Life Together*), published in 1939.

above:
Sabine and Gerhard Leibholz after their emigration, in a boarding house in Forest Hill, London.

below:
Marianne (left) and Christiane Leibholz in English school uniform. D. Bonhoeffer received these photographs during the War.

above:
Sigurdshof, façade.

below:
Log cabin in the Sigurdshof
wood near Wendisch-Tychow in
rural Pomerania.

Life in common in a difficult time

The collapse of the Confessing Church affected primarily the so-called illegal substitute clergy and theological students. The consistories made many offers to "legalize" them: they need only repeat the examinations and request the confirmation of their ordination. Bonhoeffer was drawn deeply into the conflicts which arose between the "legalists," who refused to accept the spiritual leadership of the Brotherhood Councils, and the "rejectionists." His position was clear: "Let us not deceive ourselves that we would be free on all matters of substance, once we were in the ranks of the consistory! In that position, we would abandon all inherent authority, because we would not have remained in the truth."

On November 9, 1938, the synagogues in Germany went up in flames. The night of the pogrom evoked scarcely any response among the Christians, who were confused and bruised. But Bonhoeffer had said, as early as 1935: "Only one who cries out on behalf of the Jews may also legitimately sing Gregorian chant."

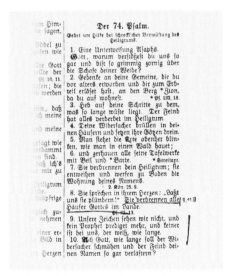

On the day of the pogrom, Bonhoeffer marked these passages in Psalm 74 in his Bible and wrote "9.11.38" beside the text.

In April, 1939, the "collective vicariate" moved into the Sigurdshof, an empty outbuilding which the landowner von Kleist had made available on the Wendisch-Tychow estate. From April 1939 to March 1940, this was the last place where Bonhoeffer was active as a theological teacher, living a spiritual life in common with others.

Refusal to do military service?

On March 6, 1939, the Military Registration Office gave a positive response to Bonhoeffer's request for a passport, and he left for England with Eberhard Bethge four days later. On his arrival in London, Bonhoeffer at once made preparations to visit Bishop Bell, this time on a personal matter. Ahead of this visit, Bonhoeffer wrote to Bell on March 25, 1939 – ten days after the German army had marched into Prague – "I am thinking of leaving Germany for a while. The main reason is the universal conscription which will affect men of my age (1906) this year. It seems to me on the grounds of conscience impossible to take part in a war under the present circumstances."

At the request of the Confessing Church, Bonhoeffer visited the "Committee for 'non-Aryan' Christians" which Bishop Bell had founded; he visited Leonard Hodgson, the general secretary of "Faith and Order"; and he met Visser 't Hooft, the general secretary of the temporary World Council of Churches, at Paddington railway station. After the War, Visser 't Hooft recalled this first meeting with Bonhoeffer: "We then had a long walk up and down the platform. He described the situation of the church and of his country. In a manner remarkably free of illusions, and sometimes almost in a prophetic tone, he spoke of the coming war which would soon be unleashed, probably in summer."

On April 18, 1939, Bonhoeffer was back in Berlin. Two days later, Hitler was honored by a thunderous birthday parade, and the legal periodical of the German Protestant church published its congratulations: "We celebrate in exultant joy the fiftieth birthday of our Führer. In him, God has given the German people a true man of wonders." One month later, Bonhoeffer was called up. Could a pastor refuse his military service? Not even in the leadership of the Confessing Church was there anyone who would have approved such a decision. His father intervened, and the Military Registration Office withdrew the order to present himself for enrollment. Bonhoeffer was given a certificate attesting that the government had no objections to his spending one year out of the country.

above:
Certification by the Military Registration Office in Schlawe in reply to the request for the issue of a passport. Signed by von Kleist, major and district military officer.

center:
Dr. George Bell, Bishop of Chichester.

below:
50th birthday of Adolf Hitler: standard bearers march past the National chancellery in Berlin, April 20, 1939.

above:
May 1939, before the departure for America, on the farm in front of the Sigurdshof buildings: from left, E. Bethge, D. Bonhoeffer, F. Onnasch, H. Korporal, H. Petermann.

center left:
Passport, valid until March 4, 1940.

center right:
Page 15 of Dietrich Bonhoeffer's passport: arrival in Croydon, June 2, 1939.

Journey to America

Union Theological Seminary in New York City gave Bonhoeffer a teaching job for the summer of 1939, and this allowed him to avoid taking up weapons in the imminent war. At the end of May, his American friend Paul Lehmann invited him also to Elmhurst College in Illinois, where he became professor of religion.

May 27, 1939

Dear Dietrich,

The news that you have been invited to give lectures in the summer course of the Union Theological Seminary in New York encourages me to put the following urgent request to you. Would you be so good as to express your willingness to lecture in the department of religion at the college here in the coming academic year, 1939-1940, and to make all the necessary preparations? I have long desired to have my students here – and others – hear your manner of reflecting on the problems of philosophy and theology. Hence I venture to include your presence in my plans and to organize similar lectures at other colleges which I know. I am certain that they will be more than keen to welcome you. The specific details can be agreed upon during your residence in Union Seminary. In the meantime, I look forward greatly to your arrival.

Yours ever sincerely,

Paul
Paul L. Lehmann Th.D.
Professor of Religion

On June 2, Dietrich Bonhoeffer's plane took off from Tempelhofer Field in Berlin. Everything had gone successfully. He was to meet his twin sister and his brother-in-law in London, then to sail over the Atlantic from Southampton on the *Bremen* with his brother Karl-Friedrich, who had been invited to lecture in Chicago. On the first postcard he wrote, while still on board his plane, Bonhoeffer noted: "My thoughts are divided between yourselves and the future. Greet all the brethren. They are at their evening service at this hour."

The short space of time in which the invitation to America had to be organized, and the necessary discretion involved in using the postal service, meant that there were different views on both sides about what was actually involved. Certainly, Bonhoeffer wanted to get away, but he did not want to shut all doors tight behind him. But how were his friends in New York to know this, when Reinhold Niebuhr had telegraphed to them that Bonhoeffer was at risk and must be rescued?

Ought Bonhoeffer to accept Henry Smith Leiper's offer of a position as pastor for German émigrés in New York? That would make it impossible for him to return to Germany. And so his unease grew: where am I needed, where ought I to be? "In all this, the only thing I miss is Germany – and the brethren … I do not understand why I am here, whether it is meaningful, whether the outcome will be worthwhile." On June 20, 1939, Bonhoeffer visited Henry Smith Leiper in the Federal Council of Churches – and rejected his job offer.

Paul Lehmann continued to try to arrange courses of lectures for Bonhoeffer at American universities, but he had already taken his decision: "I am now convinced that it was a mistake for me to come to America. I must live through this difficult epoch of our national history among the Christians of Germany. I have no right to take part in the restoration of Christian life in Germany after the war, if I do not share the tribulations of this time with my own people" (letter to R. Niebuhr, June 1939).

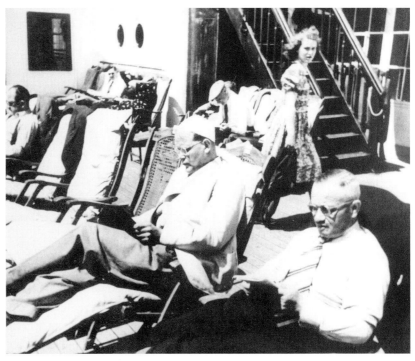

above:
Dietrich Bonhoeffer on board the
Bremen.

below left:
Reinhold Niebuhr, Professor of
Applied Christianity at the Union
Theological Seminary in New
York.

below right:
Henry Smith Leiper, executive
secretary of the Federal Council
of Churches.

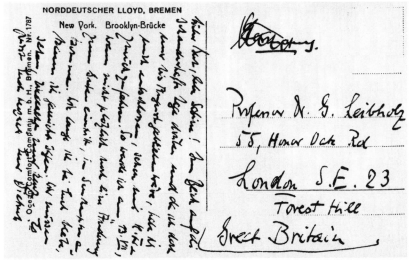

above:
Postcard to Sabine and Gerhard
Leibholz, announcing his return
from America.

below:
With his twin sister Sabine, in
the garden of the London
boarding house, July 1939.

Return to Germany

In the night of July 7–8, 1939, five weeks after Bonhoeffer had left Germany, his ship left the New York harbor. Dietrich and his brother traveled back to Europe, in the direction of war: "The journey is over. I am glad that I was over there, and happy that I am now on my way home."

Bonhoeffer spent ten days in London, staying with Gerhard and Sabine Leibholz. He met Franz Hildenbrandt, but reached Bishop Bell only by letter: "My passport expires in spring next year, and that makes it uncertain when I can return to this country."

Resistance
(1942–44)

Return to Sigurdshof

After he returned to Germany, Bonhoeffer resumed his work with the "collective vicariates" in rural Pomerania. When Hitler declared war on Poland on September 1, 1939, Bonhoeffer applied to the military bishop to be accepted for pastoral work in the army, but he received a negative reply. According to a prescription of the high command, only men who had served on the front lines in the First World War could become military chaplains.

above:
E. Bethge and D. Bonhoeffer, 1939, in front of the house at Sigurdshof.

below:
Collective vicariate, tenth course (winter 1939-1940) in front of the Sigurdshof hunting lodge. From the left: B. Kerlin, D. Bonhoeffer, Mrs. Struwe, W. Litterscheid, K.H. Probsthain, H. Birk, E. Bethge, M. Mebes, H. Vollriede, D. Muschner.

An das Reichssicherheitshauptamt
Berlin SW 11
Prinz Albrechtstr 8.

Am 4. 9. 1940 ist mir von der Staatspolizeileitstelle Köslin die Verfügung des Reichssicherheitshauptamtes IV A 4b 776/40 eröffnet worden, durch die mir ein Redeverbot für das Reichsgebiet erteilt wird. Als Grund wird"volkszersetzende Tätigkeit" angegeben.Diesen Vorwurf weise ich zurück.Es kommt für mich nach meiner gesamten Einstellung, meiner Arbeit wie auch meiner Herkunft nicht inbetracht, mich mit Kreisen identifizieren zu lassen, die den Makel eines solchen Vorwurfs mit Recht tragen.Ich gehöre mit Stolz einer Familie an, die sich um das Wohl des deutschen Volkes und Staates seit Generationen verdient gemacht hat. Zu meinen Voreltern gehört der Generalfeldmarschall Graf Kalckreuth und die beiden grossen deutschen Maler gleichen Namens; gehört der in der gesamten wissenschaftlichen Welt des vorigen Jahrhunderts bekannte Jenenser Kirchenhistoriker Karl v.Hase; die Bildhauerfamilie Cauer; mein Onkel ist der Generalleutnant Graf v.d. Goltz, der das Baltikum befreite;sein Sohn, der Staatsrat Rüdiger Graf v.d. Goltz ist mein Vetter ersten Grades;der im aktiven Heeresdienst stehende Generalleutnant v.Hase ist mein Onkel; mein Vater ist seit fast 30 Jahren ordentlicher Universitätsprofessor der Medizin in Berlin und steht bis heute in ehrenvollen Staatsämtern;seine Vorväterhaben jahrhundertelang als hochangesehene Handwerker und Ratsherren in der damaligen freien Reichsstadt Schwäbisch-Hall gelebt und noch heute zeigt man dort ihre Bilder mit Stolz in der Stadtkirche; meine Brüder und Schwäger stehen in hohen staatlichen Stellungen einer meiner Brüder fiel im Weltkrieg.Es ist das Streben aller dieser Männer und ihrer Familien gewesen, dem deutschen Staat und Volk zu jeder Stunde zu dienen und ihr Leben für diesen Dienst einzusetzen.In bewusster Bejahung dieses geistigen Erbes und dieser inneren Haltung meiner Familie kann ich den Vorwurf "volkszersetzender Tätigkeit" nicht hinnehmen...

    Darf ich nun bitten mich zu einer solchen Besprechung aufzufordern oder doch mir mitzuteilen, ob ich durch das Redeverbot auch daran gehindert sein soll, die Ergebnisse meiner gänzlich unpolitischen wissenschaftlichen Tätigkeit in kleinen Kreisen vorzutragen, also,um ein Beispiel zu nennen, vor etwa 20 - 30 interessierten Zuhörern über die Auffassung Luthers zu dieser oder jener Frage des christlichen Glaubens zu sprechen.Ich kann mir nicht denken, dass das Redeverbot in diesem Sinne ausgelegt werden soll. Ich bitte darum, mir wenigstens diese Tätigkeit zu gestatten.

Ban on speaking and obligation to register

On September 4, 1940, the National Office for Security banned Dietrich Bonhoeffer from public speaking because he was "weakening the resolve of the people." At the same time, he was obliged to register at the police station.

He could accept the ban on speaking, but not the obligation to register with the police; at all costs, he had to avoid this. Bonhoeffer wrote a letter setting out his objections. In his letter of protest, he gives particular space to the defamatory character with which this order was justified by the Office for Security, and to the patriotic reputation of his ancestors.

above:
Letter to the "Head Office for National Security" in Berlin, objecting to the ban on speaking imposed on Bonhoeffer throughout Germany.

below:
From the archives of the Gestapo, Düsseldorf office, September 20, 1940.

Between action and contemplation

In September 1940, Bonhoeffer was on Ruth von Kleist-Retzow's estate, Klein-Krössin, where he resumed work on his *Ethics*. France had capitulated, and Hitler was at the zenith of his power, a man apparently exalted above good and evil: the traditional ethical categories did not offer the possibility of opposing him. In this situation, Bonhoeffer wrote the "Confession of the Church's Sins," which includes the words: "The church confesses that it has looked on at the arbitrary use of brutal power, the bodily and psychological suffering of innumerable innocent persons, oppression, hatred, and murder, without raising its voice for the victims, without finding ways to rush to their help. It has become guilty of the life of the weakest and most defenseless brothers and sisters of Jesus Christ."

In the following years, he worked for the Confessing Church and undertook various tasks in the context of the conspiracy. Mostly, he now lived with his parents. In the Bonhoeffer and Schleicher houses in the Marienburger Allee, in Klaus Bonhoeffer's house nearby, at the Dohnanyis' home in Sakrow, as well as in Ernst von Harnack's house in Zehlendorf, the conspirators met to talk, and often to make music – this was a disguise for their meetings, but also a great joy.

In these years, Bonhoeffer's life alternated between plotting and theological meditation, between tremendous tension and relaxation. He loved chamber music and was a passionate bridge player. Sometimes, he enjoyed reading aloud the poems of Christian Morgenstern or Conrad Ferdinand Meyer.

above:
Manor in Klein-Krössin.

center:
From the "Confession of the Church's Sins."

below:
With his parents in the garden, Marienburger Allee 43.

Ettal Abbey

From the end of November 1940 to February 1941, Bonhoeffer lived in Ettal Abbey, where he also met men who played an important political role for him. At Christmas 1940, they sat up talking half the night: Father Johannes, the abbots of Metten and Ettal, the priests Dr Leiber and Dr. Zeiger, Dr. Schönhöffer from the Vatican, and Consul Schmidhuber, a member of the Abwehr office in Munich whom Bonhoeffer knew from his work.

In order to avoid the extinction of the Confessing Church due to the conscription of its members into the army or their assignment by the state to other work, Bonhoeffer attempted via intermediaries to influence the decisions taken by the Church Minister, Kerrl. In Ettal, he discussed this matter with the National Minister for Justice, Gürtner: "We spent the day together and talked about many things. He is very optimistic about Kerrl; the question is, what Kerrl himself can actually do. This is a rather urgent affair, since we hear more and more frequently that people are being assigned to other work." But one month later, Gürtner was dead.

above:
Hotel "Louis the Bavarian" in Ettal, where Bonhoeffer stayed the night.

below:
Christmas in Ettal, 1940. From left: Dietrich Bonhoeffer, Barbara von Dohnanyi, Christoph von Dohnanyi, Klaus von Dohnanyi, Eberhard Bethge.

National Justice Minister Dr .Gürtner.

Conspiracy in the Abwehr

With an unofficial commission from the group of conspirators around General Ludwig Beck, Colonel Hans Oster, and his brother-in-law von Dohnanyi, who worked under Admiral Canaris in the resistance movement, Bonhoeffer visited Switzerland for the first time from February 24 to March 24, 1941. His job was to establish new contacts with the Allies via the churches.

When he left for his second journey to Switzerland on August 29, 1941, Germany had already begun the attack on Russia. He took part in the discussion of leading Christians in the West about the goals of peace. In a memorandum on the book "The Church and the New Order" by the English general secretary of the Provisional World Council of Churches, Bonhoeffer spoke of the "total elimination of the Nazi system." The new government would emerge from a military coup and "could be formed at once. A lot would depend on whether it received the immediate support of the Allies." Visser 't Hooft made this memorandum known in England, but its significance was not understood at that time.

above left:
Major Hans Oster (General from 1943), head of the Central Office of the Abwehr (counter-espionage).

above right:
Admiral Wilhelm Canaris, head of the "Foreign/Abwehr" office in the military high command.

center left:
Dr. Hans von Dohnanyi, "special commissioner" in the department of "political advisers" in the central section of the Abwehr office.

below:
General Ludwig Beck.

Willem Visser't Hooft.

Sehr verehrter Herr Doktor!

Im Auftrage des z.Zt. verhafteten Vorsitzenden der Vorläufigen Leitung der Deutschen Evangelischen Kirche, Herrn Superintendent Lic. A l b e r t z , erlaube ich mir, Ihnen als dem Präsidenten der Schweizer Reformierten Kirchen und so an dieselben eine ebenso herzliche wie dringende Bitte auszusprechen.

Es handelt sich um die bittere Not, in der sich seit einigen Wochen viele unserer nichtarischen christlichen Brüder und Schwestern befinden. Die Vorgänge werden Ihnen bekannt sein. Seit etwa Mitte Oktober hat man damit begonnen, Nichtarier aus Berlin und anderen Städten nach dem Osten abzutransportieren. Das Ganze stellt die christlichen Kirchen vor Fragen und Nöte, denen wir nahezu hilflos gegenüberstehen.

Wir wissen, daß auch Ihnen die Hände nahezu gebunden sind. Eine Aufnahme der unmittelbar bedrohten nichtarischen Christen in die Schweiz scheint bei der Haltung der dortigen Fremdenpolizei und aus anderen Gründen unmöglich. Prof. Courvoisier-Genf mußte das vor kurzem noch einmal bestätigen. Dennoch wurde auch ihm eine Bitte, die sich auf die folgenden Fälle bezog, mitgegeben. Unsere Frage an Sie ist heute nun die, ob es bei einer dringenden Vorstellung und einem offiziellen Schritt der Schweizer Kirchen nicht doch vielleicht eine Tür für einige Wenige oder wenigstens für einen einzigen von uns besonders befürworteten Fall auftun könnte.

Den ersten und dringendsten Fall stellt Fräulein Charlotte F r i e d e n t h a l dar. Geb. am 1.12.1892 in Breslau und dort als Kind getauft, Tochter des verstorbenen Justizrates Fr. Frl. F. ist ausgebildete Wohlfahrtspflegerin. Seit Anfang 1934 steht sie in kirchlicher Arbeit, und zwar vom 31.1.34 bis 28.2.36 als stellvertretende Leiterin des Evang. Bezirkswohlfahrtsamtes / Berlin-Zehlendorf (Vorsitzender Pfarrer Niemöller); ab 2.3.36 war sie Mitarbeiterin der Vorläufigen Leitung, ab 1.10.37 persönliche Sekretärin des reformierten Mitglieds der VL, Superintendent Albertz. Ihre Mutter ist vor kurzer Zeit verstorben, die Geschwister

above:
Alphons Koechlin, 1940.

below:
Letter of request from Wilhelm
Rott to Alphons Koechlin.

"Operation 7"

While Bonhoeffer was in Switzerland, the police regulation about the marking of Jews came into effect on September 1, 1941: from September 19, all Jews must wear the star sewn onto their clothes. From the very first day, F.J. Perels and Bonhoeffer (who became seriously ill with pneumonia at the end of October and took a long time to get well again) collected all the available information about the transport of Jews, in order to pass this on to the opposition in the Army.

At the same time, preparations for "Operation 7" began. Admiral Canaris ordered that a group of between 12 and 15 Jews (originally, there were supposed to be 7) should be disguised as agents of the Abwehr office and brought to safety in Switzerland. This group included Charlotte Friedenthal, who had worked for many years for the Provisional Leadership of the Confessing Church. After consulting Bonhoeffer (who was sick) and with the help of Friedrich Justus Perels, Wilhelm Rott wrote a letter in October to Alphons Koechlin, the president of the Swiss Church Federation, asking for his help. Consul Schmidhuber of the Abwehr office in Munich took this letter into Switzerland and gave it to Koechlin. Later, in the trials in 1943, "Operation 7" was to play a dangerous role.

Antisemitic poster, 1942.

From April 10 to 18, 1942, Dietrich Bonhoeffer and Count Helmuth von Moltke traveled to Norway on Abwehr business. On April 5, all the pastors of the Norwegian Lutheran Church had resigned from office. Three days later, bishop Eivind Berggrav was arrested. It was he who had initiated this church struggle and acted as spiritual guide to the Norwegian pastors in their resistance against the German occupation.

The emissaries of the Abwehr argued that it would be imprudent of the German troops to kill the bishop, because his death would cause tremendous turmoil among the Norwegian people. Bonhoeffer and von Moltke also advised the Norwegian Lutherans to continue the church struggle which they had begun by striking, resigning from office, and formally leaving the church. Bonhoeffer saw in Norway the realization of what he himself had suggested (in vain) to his own church in 1933.

Berggrav was in fact released from prison in the same month, not because of any influence of the two emissaries from the Abwehr, but because of a decree from the National Chancellery in Berlin. The bishop was kept under house arrest until the end of the War.

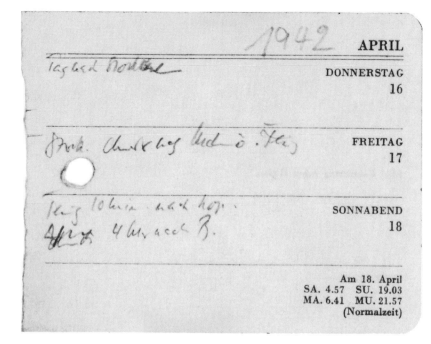

Bishop Eivind Berggrav.

above:
A page from Bonhoeffer's pocket diary with notes concerning his trip to Norway.

below:
Helmuth James von Moltke's passport.

17. V. 42.

Lieber Herr Professor!

Verzeihen Sie bitte, wenn das, was ich nun schreibe, Unsinn und nicht der Rede wert ist. Aber fragen muss ich nun doch, weil mir die Sache zu sehr nachgeht: Als ich in der vorigen Woche in Zürich zum ersten Mal hörte, mein Aufenthalt hier sei Ihnen 'wegen der Aufträge unheimlich', habe ich einfach gelacht; als ich kurz darauf in Zürich zum zweiten Mal auf diese angebliche Äusserung von Ihnen stiess, habe ich gedacht, es wäre am richtigsten, überhaupt nicht darauf einzugehen. Nun höre ich dasselbe bereits zum zweiten Mal hier in Genf, und nachdem ich es mir ein paar Tage lang überlegt habe, möchte ich Ihnen das einfach sagen. Ich bin mir klar darüber, dass es in so engen Kreisen viel dummes Gerede gibt und dass es gut möglich ist, dass es sich nur um irgendeine aufgebauschte Sache handelt. Wenn es aber nicht so wäre, dann wüsste ich jetzt wirklich nicht, was ich dazu sagen sollte. In einer Zeit, in der so vieles einfach auf persönlichem Vertrauen stehen muss, ist ja alles vorbei, wenn Misstrauen aufkommt.

Basel,den 17.Mai 1942.

Lieber Herr Bonhoeffer!

Nun haben wir die Bescherung! Lassen Sie sich vor allem sagen,dass auch wir lachen über diese Sache,wenn auch mit einem weinenden Auge, denn dass solcher Tumult überhaupt entstehen konnte,ist Grund genug betrübt zu sein und will auch in seiner Weise ernst genommen sein als "Zeichen der Zeit". Also: Karl Barth hat Ihnen nie einen Augenblick misstraut oder,um ganz exakt zu sein,hat,als ihm eine Frage aufstieg hinsichtlich der Möglichkeit Ihrer Reisen,diese Frage Ihnen ja gleich direkt gestellt. Sollte es in diesen Tagen zu irgend einer zu den Freunden hin ausgesprochenen Frage gekommen sein(auf eine diesbezügliche Anfrage hin,wieso Sie denn diese Freiheit haben? (eine Frage,die uns wieder und wieder gestellt wird),so könnte sie der einzig reale Untergrund für die nun anscheinend laufende Aeusserung,Ihr Hiersein sei"ihm unheimlich wegen Ihrer Aufträge" sein.Er selbst erinnert sich nicht,darüber gesprochen zu haben und ich habe nichts dergleichen gehört. Und als dann im Gespräch mit Ihnen auch für ihn selbst diese Frage beantwortet war, hat er nur und nach allen Seiten hin Ihr Kommen bejaht.Dass auch das wieder und wieder nötig wurde und wird,das zeigt Ihnen,wie ängstlich und wie misstrauisch man hier mit "uns" geworden ist. Vor einigen Wochen hat die Fremdenpolizei bei Karl Barth angefragt,ob er für Ihre Einreise gut stehen könne,er hat das bedenkenlos getan und daraufhin wurde die Erlaubnis erteilt. Sie sehen also: die Sache ist gegenstandslos. Auch durch den engeren Freundeskreis (Thurneysen,Vischer) ging einmal ein kleines Staunen über Ihre Freizügigkeit,es wurde aber nach dem Gespräch von Karl mit Ihnen restlos beseitigt und als wir in diesen Tagen beiden erzählten,dass Sie hier seien,war die Antwort eine ganz eindeutig erfreute. Sie können also auch dorthin ohne den leisesten Unterton von Betrübtheit denken.

A visit to Karl Barth

Bonhoeffer's third visit to Switzerland probably began on May 11, 1942. This time, a number of questions hung in the air: Where had he got his passport, his visa, and his Swiss francs? What kind of commissions was he undertaking on behalf of officers in Hitler's army? And what was this "other Germany" he was talking about? Rumors reached Bonhoeffer that Karl Barth did not trust him, and he reacted at once, writing to Barth on May 17:

Please excuse me if what I am now writing is nonsense and not worth mentioning, but I must put this question, since the matter concerns me too closely. When I heard for the first time, in Zurich last week, that you found my stay here "highly suspicious, because of the commissions" I was undertaking, I laughed ... But now I hear the same thing for the second time here in Geneva, and after thinking it over for a couple of days, I want to let you know ... that in a time in which so much must depend on personal trust, everything is over if distrust arises.

Dietrich Bonhoeffer and Karl Barth, 1942.

Karl Barth's answer, brought by Charlotte von Kirschbaum, was unambiguous: he approved of Bonhoeffer's visit and was happy that he was in Switzerland. Bonhoeffer visited Barth, but then came the news that Bishop Bell was to visit Sweden. Time was short, and Bonhoeffer broke off his stay in Switzerland.

left:
Exchange of letters between Bonhoeffer and Karl Barth, May 17, 1942.

Meeting with Bishop Bell in Sigtuna

In Berlin, General Ludwig Beck, Hans Oster, and Hans von Dohnanyi decided to send Dietrich Bonhoeffer to Sweden, asking Bishop Bell to get in touch with the British government with the request that, when the planned coup in Germany took place, their armed forces "would not exploit this opportunity for an attack, but would give the new government a certain period of time to clear up the situation in the country" (Christine von Dohnanyi).

Bonhoeffer was authorized to inform Bishop Bell confidentially of the names of those who were planning the coup. On May 31, he met the bishop in Sigtuna with Dr. Hans Schönfeld, who had also come to Sweden (independently of Bonhoeffer) as the emissary of a second resistance group connected to the Foreign Ministry and the "Kreisau circle." When he was alone with the bishop, Bonhoeffer told him the names of the plotters: Beck, Hammerstein, Goerdeler, Leuschner, Kaiser; caution was advised with regard to another name, Schacht.

When Foreign Minister Anthony Eden received Bell, he gave him a negative response: "Although I do not in the least wish to call into question the accuracy of your informants, I am convinced that is not in the national interest to send them any answer whatever." On July 23, Bishop Bell sent a telegram to Geneva: "Interest undoubted – but greatly regret no answer possible. Bell."

above left:
Bishop George Bell.

above right:
Hans Schönfeld.

center:
House of Harry Johansson, head of the Scandinavian Ecumenical Institute, where Bonhoeffer and Bell met in Sigtuna.

below:
Guest book in Sigtuna: George Cicestr (Bishop Bell), Manfred Björkquist (head of the Academy in Sigtuna), DB (Bonhoeffer used only his initials, since he was on a secret mission), Nils Ehrenström (Ecumenical Council in Geneva).

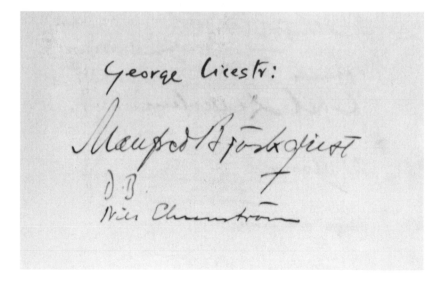

above:
"To the pastors and office-bearers" – a letter to the clergy about the "immediate post-coup program."

center:
Friedrich Justus Perels.

below:
Notes made by Bonhoeffer in preparation for a meeting of the "Freiburg circle," dated Tuesday, November 17. First line: "economic question Eucken, von Dietze, Bauer (Karrenberg)"; second line: "Law of the state, internal decalogue."

Immediate post-coup program

Bonhoeffer joined the legal adviser to the Confessing Church, Friedrich Justus Perels, in planning an "immediate post-coup program." They wanted at all costs to prevent "the reactionary circles of the former general superintendents and the bureaucracy of the church offices from regaining their control of the church."

Bonhoeffer drafted a proclamation from the pulpits and a letter to the clergy, which said: "We call you to reorder your lives. For long enough, we have suffered because each one has gone his own way and has separated himself from his brother. This was not the Spirit of Christ, but a self-opinionated, defiant spirit which took the easy path."

When he was arrested, the military lawyer Roeder found a draft of a new ordering of church life, entitled "Ending the Church Struggle." This title allowed Bonhoeffer during his trial to conceal the true intention of this text.

He also got in touch with the authors of the "Frankfurt Memorandum," which was composed between September 1942 and January 1943 and contains reflections on the new ordering of Germany after the War. A sheet of paper with notes by Bonhoeffer for a discussion in November 1943 has survived; but by that date, he had already been arrested.

Engagement

In June 1942, Bonhoeffer was the guest of Ruth von Kleist-Retzow in Klein Krössin, where he met again her granddaughter, Maria von Wedemeyer. He was enchanted by this eighteen-year-old, who had just graduated from high school. Unlike Maria's mother Ruth, who was married to the landowner Hans von Wedemeyer in Pätzig in the Neumark district, the countess supported this love and brought the two of them together in the hospital in Berlin where she had a cataract operation.

When Dietrich and Maria became engaged in January 1943, she accepted that she would have to wait a long time until their engagement became public knowledge, and they could marry: her father had died a few months earlier on the eastern front. Dietrich's arrest put an end to these plans, and Maria's mother announced the engagement in June of 1943.

When Dietrich entered her family circle in this way, Ruth von Kleist-Retzow gave him the biography of her father-in-law, Hans Hugo von Kleist-Retzow, an important politician in the time of Bismarck, with the following dedication: "To Dietrich Bonhoeffer from Ruth von Kleist, née Countess of Zedlitz and Trützschler: I am happy, dear Dietrich, to whom I owe insights of decisive importance for my life, on this day on which you are entering visibly our family, that I can give you this book. Its subject is a man who bequeathed a tangible blessing in which you too are now included – Klein Krössin (Kieckow), June 24, 1943."

above:
Tranquil days in Pomerania. With Ruth and Konstantin von Kleist-Retzow in Kieckow, 1942.

center:
Maria von Wedemeyer (photographed in 1942).

below:
Pätzig 1944: confirmation of Christine von Wedemeyer (third from left: Maria von Wedemeyer).

Crisis in the Munich Abwehr

At the beginning of September 1942, Dietrich Bonhoeffer began preparations for new journeys to the Balkans and Switzerland. On October 2, he took the train to Munich, in order to get the endorsement necessary for foreign travel.

Just at this moment, a crisis broke out in the Munich Abwehr office: the customs office in Prague had discovered currency irregularities on the part of a man who claimed to be acting on behalf of the office in Munich. Consul Schmidhuber was arrested, and Josef Müller was interrogated. Damaging statements were made in connection with currency transactions which had been necessary in order to realize "Operation 7" – the secret transport of Jews to Switzerland. The names of Hans von Dohnanyi and Dietrich Bonhoeffer were mentioned in the protocol of the investigation. Why was this Protestant pastor allegedly essential to the military organization of the Abwehr? The conflict between the National Security Office and the counter-espionage Abwehr office intensified.

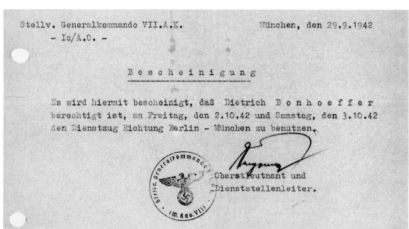

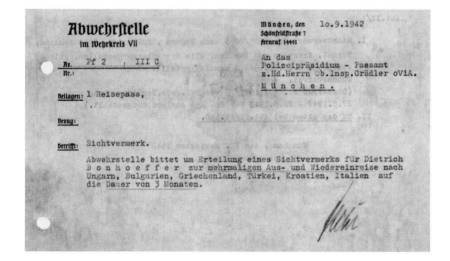

above left:
Consul Wilhelm Schmidhuber, member of the Abwehr office in Munich.

above right:
Dr. Josef Müller, lawyer and contact man between the Abwehr group and the Vatican.

center:
Permit for the use of the official train.

below:
Request by the Abwehr office for the issue of an endorsement permitting Bonhoeffer to travel abroad.

First attempted assassination

In November 1942, the Allies landed in North Africa; two months later, Stalingrad fell, and Roosevelt and Churchill demanded "unconditional surrender." The German military situation became worse and worse, and now defeat seemed imminent.

On March 13, 1943, Hitler was due to visit the Central Army group at the front in Smolensk. This gave an opportunity to assassinate him.

Hans von Dohnanyi flew to Smolensk, carrying in his bag a special explosive for Tresckow and Schlabrendorff. Eberhard Bethge drove von Dohnanyi in Karl Bonhoeffer's car (which was still licenced, despite the wartime restrictions) to the railway station to get the night train. He knew nothing about the explosive in his passenger's bag.

When Hitler flew back on March 13, the package with the activated timebombs was on board. But Hitler landed unscathed. The bombs had failed to work.

above left:
Major-General Henning von Tresckow.

above right:
Dr. Hans von Dohnanyi, head of the special section in the department.

center:
Lieutenant Colonel Fabian von Schlabrendorff.

below:
Professor Dr. Karl Bonhoeffer getting into his car.

above and center:
Summons to D. Bonhoeffer to present himself for enrollment in the Military Registration Office in Munich, March 13, 1943.

below:
Hitler leaves the "Zeughaus", March 21, 1943.

Second attempted assassination

On the same day, March 13, 1943, Bonhoeffer received a new summons from the Military Registration Office in Munich to present himself for enrollment. One last time, General Oster used his special powers to free Bonhoeffer from this requirement – the plans for a coup could now continue.

On Sunday, March 21, the plotters had a new opportunity, when Hitler visited an exhibition of military booty in the "Zeughaus" in Berlin. Major von Gersdorff, a counter-espionage officer in the Central Army group, was waiting for him. He carried bombs on his own body, in order to kill himself along with Hitler.

On the morning of that day, the family and all the grandchildren practiced the birthday cantata in the Schleichers' house to celebrate the 75th birthday of Dietrich's father. Dietrich sat at the piano, Klaus played the cello, Rüdiger Schleicher the violin, and Hans von Dohnanyi was in the choir. His car stood ready outside the door. Christine von Dohnanyi whispered to her sister Ursula: "It will go up any minute now!" But the minutes passed, and the telephone remained silent. What had happened? Hitler did not keep to the planned schedule, but left the exhibition after only ten minutes. Major von Gersdorff never had the chance to get close to him.

Arrest

On April 5, one week after the birthday celebrations, during which Karl Bonhoeffer received the Goethe Medal with a certificate signed by Hitler, Dietrich Bonhoeffer, Hans and Christine von Dohnanyi, and Josef and Maria Müller were arrested.

right:
Bestowal of the Goethe Medal on Prof. Dr. Karl Bonhoeffer. From left: Prof. Zutt, Prof. Bonhoeffer, Prof. Krenz, Klaus and Karl-Friedrich Bonhoeffer.

Together for the last time: the Bonhoeffer family on Karl Bonhoeffer's 75th birthday, March 31, 1943, five days before Dietrich was arrested.
Front row, sitting (from left): Karl-Friedrich Bonhoeffer, Paula Bonhoeffer with Walter Bonhoeffer on her knees, Karl Bonhoeffer with Andreas Dress, Ursula Schleicher; standing, front row (from left): Dietrich Bonhoeffer, Christine von Dohnanyi, Christoph von Dohnanyi, Friedrich Bonhoeffer, Christine Schleicher, Susanne Dress, in front of her: Cornelie Bonhoeffer, Barbara von Dohnanyi, Michael Dress, Dorothee Schleicher, Karl Bonhoeffer, Klaus von Dohnanyi, Thomas Bonhoeffer, Rüdiger Schleicher, Emmi Bonhoeffer, Klaus Bonhoeffer, Walter Dress; in the background: left Eberhard Bethge, to the left in front of the door Prof. and Mrs. Zutt, at the right doorpost Prof. Creutzfeld and Prof. Sauerbruch, on the extreme right Mrs. Czeppan and Friedrich Justus Perels.

Who can hold out?

The great masquerade of evil has sown confusion in all ethical concepts. For one whose background is in the ethical concepts handed down in our tradition, it is absolutely confusing to see evil appear in the form of light, of good deeds, of historical necessity, of social justice; for a Christian whose life is nourished by the Bible, it is the confirmation of the abysmal badness of evil.

We see clearly the failure of those "r e a s o n a b l e" persons who believe – with the best of intentions, but a naïve failure to recognize reality – that a little reason suffices to repair the organism that has come unstuck. Since they cannot see properly, they want to be fair to all parties. This means that they are crushed under the collision of the opposing sides, without achieving anything at all. Disappointed in the unreasonableness of the world, they believe that they are condemned to unfruitfulness. They step wearily aside, or fall a hapless prey to the one who is stronger.

Even more terrible is the collapse of all ethical f a n a t i c i s m. The fanatic thinks that he can oppose the power of evil with the purity of a principle, but he is like a bull who charges against the red cloth instead of against the man who is holding it. He gets entangled in pointless matters, and falls a prey to the one who is cleverer. The man of c o n s c i e n c e puts up a solitary fight against the situations which force him to take a decision, but the sheer scale of the conflicts in which he must make his choice – advised and supported by nothing but his own conscience – lacerates him. The countless respectable and seductive disguises in which evil draws near to him make his conscience timid and uncertain, until he is finally content to have an appeased conscience rather than a good one – in other words, until he tells lies to his own conscience, in order that he may not utterly despair. For a man whose only support is his conscience can never understand that a bad conscience can actually be healthier and stronger than a conscience which is deceived.

The sure path of d u t y seems to offer a way out of the confusing thickets of potential decisions. Here, that which is commanded is seen to be the most certain path, since it is the commander who bears responsibility for the command, not the one who carries it out. If, however, we accept this limitation to the requirements of duty, we will never dare to perform the action on our own responsibility which alone can strike evil in its heart and overcome it. Ultimately, the man of duty will be obliged to do the duty he owes even to the devil himself.

From "After ten years," a report Bonhoeffer wrote at Christmas 1942.
right:
D. Bonhoeffer, 1939, outside the house in Sigurdshof.

Tegel
(1943–45)

Arrest and life in a prison cell

Towards midday on April 5, 1943, Bonhoeffer tried to call his sister, Christine von Dohnanyi, from Marienburger Allee, but the telephone was answered by a man. He knew at once: their house was being searched! Without disturbing his parents, who were sleeping, he went up to his attic room and examined his writing desk one last time. Then he waited in the neighboring house, with his sister Ursula Schleicher. About 4 o'clock, his father came across and said: "Two men want to talk to you in your room!" Shortly afterwards, Colonel Roeder of the Military Judicial Tribunal and Gestapo Commissioner Sonderegger drove off with him.

Dietrich spent a cold night in the admissions cell of the military prison for those awaiting trial, Tegel. He found the stench too strong, and could not bring himself to use the blankets which lay on his plank bed. From the neighboring cell, he heard loud weeping. In the morning, dry bread was thrown onto the floor through a crack in the door. The staff were instructed not to speak to the newly admitted prisoners. It was only on April 14 that he was able to send a letter to his parents; after this, he was allowed to write every ten days. His father asked to speak to him, but this petition was refused on April 20.

Bonhoeffer's first cell was on the fourth floor. Later, he was put in cell 92 on the third floor. For one and a half years, he lived in a room two meters by three, with a plank bed, a pin board on the wall, a stool and a bucket. The heavy wooden door had a slit through which he could be observed, but he could not see out. On the other side, there was a skylight, too high for him to see anything.

Initially, he found life in the cell in Tegel a tremendous torture. The prisoners had neither soap nor a change of underwear. Earlier in his life, he had voluntarily spent time on his own, but this was different: in the first period, he was kept in strict isolation, and the guards were forbidden to speak to the "political" prisoners. This was much harsher than a spiritual "retreat" in silence. In a surviving note from his first weeks in prison, we read: "Suicide, not because I am conscious of guilt, but because I am basically already dead. A full stop. The end."

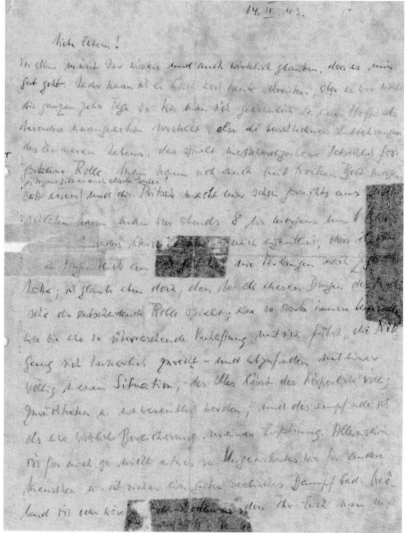

left page:

above:
Military prison, Berlin-Tegel
(X = Bonhoeffer's first cell).

below:
First letter to his parents, April
14, 1943 (excerpt).

right page:

above:
The cell in Tegel.

below:
Undated note, from a notebook
in which, on May 8, 1943, his
father wrote down the exact
contents of a food package
which he had brought into the
prison for his son.

Dietrich Bonhoeffer was afraid that he might not be able to endure ill treatment or to resist the tricks of his interrogators, and that he might reveal the names of friends who were continuing the conspiracy outside. Might not suicide actually be his duty?

In the following period, there are no such notes. In a letter of November 18, 1943, Bonhoeffer writes: "At the beginning, I was also worried by the question whether it is truly for the sake of Christ's cause that I am causing you all such distress. But I soon dismissed this question as a temptation, and became certain that my task was precisely to survive this borderline situation, with all the problems it entails."

Discontent – tension
impatience
yearning
boredom
night – deeply alone
indifference
eagerness to do something, variety,
novelty
dullness, tiredness, sleeping – to be
fought by harsh discipline

letting the imagination run riot, distor-
tion of the past and the future

suicide, not because I am conscious of
guilt, but because I am
basically already dead.
A full stop. The end.

Does the memory work better for happy
impressions?
Why is this so? A pain in the past
is seen as something that has been
overcome,
only pains that are not overcome
(unforgiven guilt)
are always fresh and tormenting to the
memory.
Overcoming in prayer

Wedding sermon and thoughts about baptism – from a prison cell

Bonhoeffer was not present at the wedding of his friend Eberhard Bethge and Dietrich's niece Renate, née Schleicher, on May 15, 1943. In Tegel prison, he wrote the "Wedding Sermon from a Prison Cell." A year later, he wrote his "Thoughts on the Christening Day of Dietrich Wilhelm Rüdiger Bethge," which Sergeant Linke brought to Marienburger Allee 43. Linke was one of the guards whom Bonhoeffer trusted. These men secretly posted letters from the inmates and delivered coded messages.

Wedding of Eberhard and Renate Bethge, née Schleicher, May 15, 1943.

Baptism of Dietrich Bethge: with his great-grandparents in the garden, Marienburger Allee 42.

above:
Bonhoeffer's "Thoughts on the Christening Day of Dietrich Wilhelm Rüdiger Bethge," 1944.

below:
In the Schleichers' house (3rd from left: Sergeant Linke; far right: Maria von Wedemeyer).

Today, you are baptized as a Christian. All the great words of the Christian proclamation will be spoken over you, and Jesus Christ's commandment to baptize will be carried out for you, although you do not understand anything of what is going on. But we ourselves are thrown back to the very beginnings of our understanding. Reconciliation and redemption, rebirth and Holy Spirit, love of enemies, cross and resurrection, life in Christ and the imitation of Christ – all this is so difficult and so far-off that we scarcely dare any more to speak of it. In the traditional words and actions, we sense something completely new and revolutionary, but we cannot yet grasp it and express it. This is our own fault. Our church, which in these years has struggled only for its own self-preservation as if that were an end in itself, is incapable of being the bearer of the word that can reconcile and redeem human beings and the world.

This is why our earlier words must lose their power and fall silent, and our Christianity today will consist in only two things: in praying and in the actions of that one among human beings who is righteous. All thinking, speaking, and organizing in Christian affairs must be reborn of this prayer and this conduct.

By the time you have grown up, the form of the church will have altered greatly. The melting-down has not yet stopped, and every attempt to help the church to achieve a new organizational power will be merely a postponement of its conversion and purification. It is not our task to predict the day – but the day will come – when people will once again be called to utter the Word of God in such a way that the world is changed and renewed under this Word. It will be a new language, perhaps completely unreligious, but liberating and redeeming, like the language of Jesus, so that people are outraged by it – and yet are conquered by its power – the language of a new righteousness and truth, the language which proclaims the peace of God with human beings and the approach of his kingdom. "And they will wonder and be astonished at all the good and all the peace that I will give them" (Jer 33:9). Until then, Christians will lead a quiet and hidden life, but there will be people who pray and do what is right and wait for God's own time. May you be one of them, and may these words one day apply to you: "The path of the righteous shines like the light, which becomes brighter and brighter until the full light of day" (Prov 4:18).

above left:
Dr. Roeder of the Supreme Military Tribunal (caricature by Hans von Dohnanyi).

above right:
Military Judge Dr. Karl Sack.

below:
Karl Ludwig Freiherr von Guttenberg, Justus Delbrück, Hans von Dohnanyi (photograph taken in 1941 or 1942 on the birthday of Hans Oster).

The investigation of Hans von Dohnanyi

The main accused was Hans von Dohnanyi. By prosecuting him, the National Security Office hoped to strike a blow against the entire Abwehr under Admiral Canaris. The other prisoners, Josef Müller and initially also Christine von Dohnanyi and Maria Müller, were accomplices in the case of Dohnanyi. This is why Bonhoeffer's trial depended on the state of the proceedings against his brother-in-law: he was happy when things speeded up, but he complained about delays. Family and friends helped spread a net of disguise to cover up the real actions, and this net was stable until seriously incriminating material was found in a reserve depot of the Abwehr in Zossen, two months after the catastrophe of July 20, 1944.

A tough struggle began between Hans von Dohnanyi and Dr. Roeder, who was entrusted with the investigation. The help of Judge Karl Sack, the head of the military judicial department, proved decisive.

Hans von Dohnanyi was not simply defenseless before his accusers: influential friends, especially Canaris, came to his aid. Canaris oversaw the attempts made by their friends to coordinate the statements of the prisoners, who were kept in isolation from another; in the Abwehr headquarters, this task fell above all to Karl Ludwig Freiherr von Guttenberg and to Justus Delbrück, the brother of Emmi Bonhoeffer. It was von Dohnanyi himself who had got these two men positions in Canaris's department.

On November 23, 1943, a firebomb hit von Dohnanyi's cell, and the guards found him unable to speak and with his face paralyzed. Dr. Sack had him moved to the Charité hospital, where, under the protection of his physician, Sauerbruch, he was allowed to receive visits from his family and a few friends. On January 12, 1944, Karl Bonhoeffer wrote to Prof. Sauerbruch about a fictitious worsening of von Dohnanyi's illness. The aim was to keep him as long as possible out of the clutches of his investigators.

What does it mean to tell the truth?

The case against Bonhoeffer was investigated from April to July, 1943. This was the period of interrogations, and it was vital that the prisoners succeeded in harmonizing their statements. Every lapse in attention, every difference in the stories they told, could have tremendous consequences.

News was brought from one prison to another by close family members, who marked passages on pages of the books which Bonhoeffer – as a prisoner still awaiting trial – was permitted to read. For example, Bonhoeffer asked to read Paul Kirn's book *Aus der Frühzeit des Nationalgefühls*. If the name of its owner, D. Bonhoeffer, was underlined, this meant that on every second page – starting from the back – he had made a little point with a pencil over one single letter. These letters, taken together, transmitted the message which was vital at that particular point in the interrogations, e.g. "No contact with ..." The family spent hours poring over the task of decipherment, so that the messages could be brought to von Dohnanyi in the Lehrter Straße, or to Perels and Seck, or to Delbrück and Canaris.

The investigations against Bonhoeffer concentrated on his assignment to the Abwehr, on "Operation 7," his travels at the service of the conspiracy, and on the dispensation of clergy of the Confessing Church from military service. During this period, he worked on his defense; he drafted letters to Roeder in which he completed or corrected his statements during an interrogation. The central point was to cover up what the conspiracy had actually aimed at doing. Finally, Bonhoeffer gave a theological account of his own life, as we see in the fragmentary essay entitled: "What does it mean to tell the truth?" which he wrote during these months.

It was not possible to maintain the original charge of high treason; supporting evidence would not emerge until after July 20, 1944. For now, Bonhoeffer was accused of weakening the resolve of the armed forces. On September 16, 1943, Dr. Wergin, a lawyer friend of Klaus Bonhoeffer whom Dietrich had chosen as his defense counsel, was confirmed in this position by the National Military Tribunal.

left:
Front cover of P. Kirn, *Aus der Frühzeit des Nationalgefühls*, Leipzig 1943.

center:
National Military Tribunal: Admission of lawyer Dr. Kurt Wergin as Bonhoeffer's defense counsel.

below:
Second draft of "What does it mean to tell the truth?" (handwritten original, in ink).

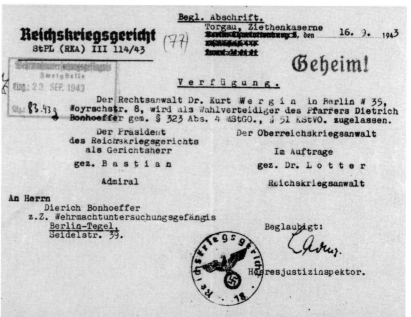

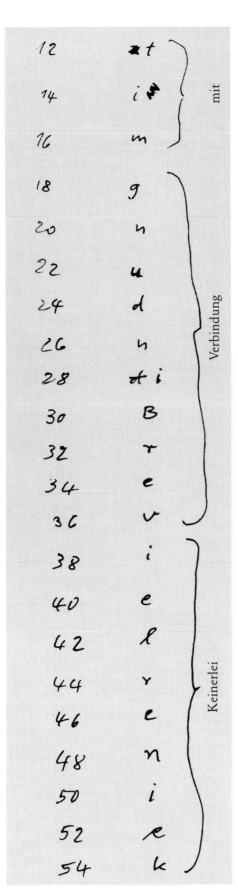

12	t	} mit
14	i	
16	m	
18	g	} Verbindung
20	n	
22	u	
24	d	
26	n	
28	ti	
30	B	
32	r	
34	e	
36	v	
38	i	} Keinerlei
40	e	
42	l	
44	r	
46	e	
48	n	
50	i	
52	e	
54	k	

left:
Decipherment of the code used by Bonhoeffer to coordinate the statements made under interrogation: "no kind of contact with."

below:
Charges laid against Dietrich Bonhoeffer, September 1, 1943.

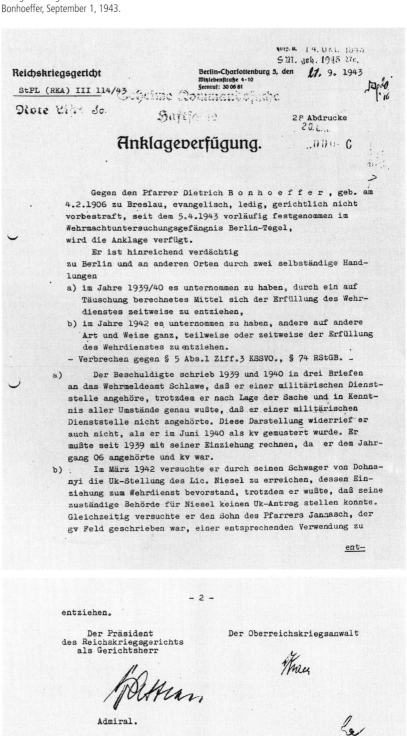

Letters from the cell, reading and writing

In Tegel, Bonhoeffer wrote letters to his parents, to his fiancée, and to his friend. The letters he wrote gave him great joy, and he looked forward to communicating in this way; they made a tremendous impression on the readers. Between November 1943 and August 1944, Eberhard Bethge, now serving as a solider in Italy, received letters amounting to a total of 200 closely-written pages, all of them smuggled out of prison. They form the basis of his book *Letters and Papers from Prison* which found a worldwide echo.

When the interrogations became less intensive, Bonhoeffer extended his daily program of activity by reading philosophical, historical, literary, and theological works that he received from his parents or from the prison library, or by exchanging books with other prisoners. He was delighted to discover Adalbert Stifter: "With my reading, I am living completely in the nineteenth century. In these months, I have read Gotthelf, Stifter, Immermann, Fontane, and Keller with a new admiration."

In April 1944, Dr. Sack informed Bonhoeffer that he ought not to expect a speedy change in his circumstances: no date had been set for his trial. This news started Bonhoeffer off on the most important creative period in his time in Tegel.

He wrote literary works and poems of his own and began to write the story of a bourgeois family of his age in the form of a play and novel. "My life in here is accompanied almost daily by this encounter with the past, the attempt to hold it fast and to take hold of it anew – and above all, by the fear of losing it." The "experience of the past, whether it was one hour ago or years ago – the two quickly merge into one another – is a task to which I return repeatedly."

The first light of morning creeps through my window
pale and gray.
A light wind passes across my forehead
with the mild warmth of summer.
"A summer day!" I say, "a lovely summer day!"
What will it bring me?
Then I hear quick, restrained steps outside.
They suddenly stop near me.
I turn cold and hot,
I know – oh, I know!
A low voice reads something, cold and incisive tones:
Get a grip on yourself, brother, it will be over soon, soon, soon!
I hear you walking courageously, with proud steps.
You no longer see the present moment,
you see future times.
I go with you, brother, to that place,
and I hear your last words:
"Brother, when the sun sets for me,
live for me!"

center:
"Nocturnal Voices in Tegel" (excerpt). Original manuscript, ink. Written in June 1944.

above right:
Eberhard Bethge
as a soldier in Italy.

center right:
W. Dilthey, "Das Erlebnis und die Dichtung," a present on Bonhoeffer's 38th birthday with a dedication in his father's handwriting: "On February 4, 1944, for solitary hours. F[ather]."

below right:
Bonhoeffer's reading in prison: "Thoughts and Reflections" by Adalbert Stifter.

I am continually driven to ponder the question what Christianity or Christ really is for us today. The age in which one could say this to people in words – whether the words of theology or those of piety – is past; the age of spirituality and of the conscience is likewise past, indeed the age of religion in any form. We are entering a completely religionless age. It is no longer possible for human beings, as they now are, to be religious. Even those who sincerely call themselves "religious" do not practice religion in any way; presumably, they attach a wholly different meaning to the word "religious."

All our nineteen hundred years of Christian proclamation and theology are however based on the "religious a priori" of human beings. "Christianity" has always been one form (perhaps the true form) of "religion." But if it one day becomes clear that this "a priori" is simply non-existent, but was a historically conditioned form of human expression which belongs to the past, so that human beings truly become radically religionless – and I believe that this is more or less the case already (or else why does this war, unlike all previous wars, not call forth a "religious" reaction?) – what does this imply for "Christianity"? All that we have known as "Christianity" up to now loses its foundations, and there are only a few "last Mohicans" or a few intellectually dishonest persons with whom we can make a "religious" contact.

Are these supposed to be the few elect? Ought we to swoop down – full of zeal, of pique, or of indignation – on this dubious group of people, in order to sell them our wares? Ought we to fall on a few unhappy persons in their hour of weakness and perform a kind of religious rape on them? If we do not want to do this, and if we must ultimately judge the western form of Christianity to be only a preliminary stage before the arrival of total religionlessness, what kind of situation is that for us, for the church?

How can Christ be Lord even of the religionless? Are there religionless Christians? If religion is only one garment of Christianity – and this garment too has looked very different in the various epochs of history – what then is a religionless Christianity?

Outlines of a new theology

In his book on discipleship, Bonhoeffer had written: "An insight cannot be separated from the existence in which it is acquired." In Tegel too, the prisoner remained aware of this connection: "It has been an experience of inestimable value, to learn to see the great events of world history from below, from the perspective of those excluded, suspected, ill treated, the powerless, the oppressed, the scorned – in short, from the perspective of the sufferers."

Bonhoeffer acted to help many of his fellow inmates. He wrote a "Memorandum about an airraid alarm," demanding new measures to protect the prisoners. He wrote a "Report on prison conditions" describing the humiliating methods of punishment, the diet, and the living situation in Tegel, in the hope that this document would reach his uncle, General Paul von Hase, in the Commandant's office in Berlin. He wrote letters of complaint on behalf of other prisoners and used his father's professional contacts to obtained psychiatric reports which could be employed in their future defense. He prayed with those condemned to death, accompanying them on their final journey.

In Tegel, Bonhoeffer pondered what the church could be in this world, and he developed the idea of a "religionless Christianity." The world has grown mature and can do without the "working hypothesis of a God": the world is self-explanatory. On July 16, 1944, he wrote to Eberhard Bethge: "God teaches us that we must live as persons whose life succeeds without God. The God who is with us is the God who abandons us."

above:
In the courtyard of the Military Prison in Tegel, with captured officers of the Italian Air Force, early summer of 1944. From left: Mario Gilli, Dante Curcio, First Sergeant Napp, who had the photographs taken, Dietrich Bonhoeffer, Edmondo Tognelli.
below:
Letter, April 30, 1944.

Hoping for a coup d'état

When Dietrich's uncle, General Paul von Hase, the Commandant of the city of Berlin, visited him in the guardroom in Tegel at the end of June 1944, Bonhoeffer's hopes for a coup d'état intensified. The preparations for the assassination attempt in the East Prussian headquarters of the Führer now entered the decisive phase, and it seemed that they would not have to wait long for him to be overthrown: the conspiracy had reached its goal. Three weeks later, on July 20, von Hase issued the necessary military commands for the elimination of the National Socialist dictatorship.

In the days before the imminent attempt on Hitler's life, Bonhoeffer reflected once more on the meaning of his life. Several months earlier, he had touched on this subject: "I often wonder who I really am ... one knows oneself less than ever, nor does one attach any importance to this question. I sense an ever deeper boredom with psychological questions and a disinclination to analyze my soul. I believe that this is why Stifter and Gotthelf have become so important to me. There are more important things than self-knowledge" (letter of December 15, 1943).

At the beginning of the decisive month, July 1944, he took up this theme in the poem "Who am I?"

Uncle Paul was here, and had me called down at once. Maetz and Maass were there too, and he remained for five hours! He had five bottles of sparkling wine brought up – something doubtless unique in the chronicles of this house – and he was generous and friendly to a degree I would hardly have thought possible. I imagine he wanted to make it very clear what he thinks of me, and what he expects of the timorous and pedantic Maetz.

I was impressed by this independence, which would surely be unthinkable in a civilian. I recall too a nice story he told me. At the battle of St. Privat, a wounded officer cadet cried in a loud voice: "I am wounded; God save the king!" And General von Löwenfeld, who was also wounded, replied, "Be quiet, Mr. Cadet. We die quietly here!" – I am waiting eagerly to see what effects this visit will have, i.e., on the way people view the situation.

above:
Letter, June 30, 1944.

center:
General Paul von Hase, city Commandant of Berlin, with the Japanese Foreign Minister Matsuoka, March 27, 1941, in Berlin.

below:
Paul von Hase before the People's Court.

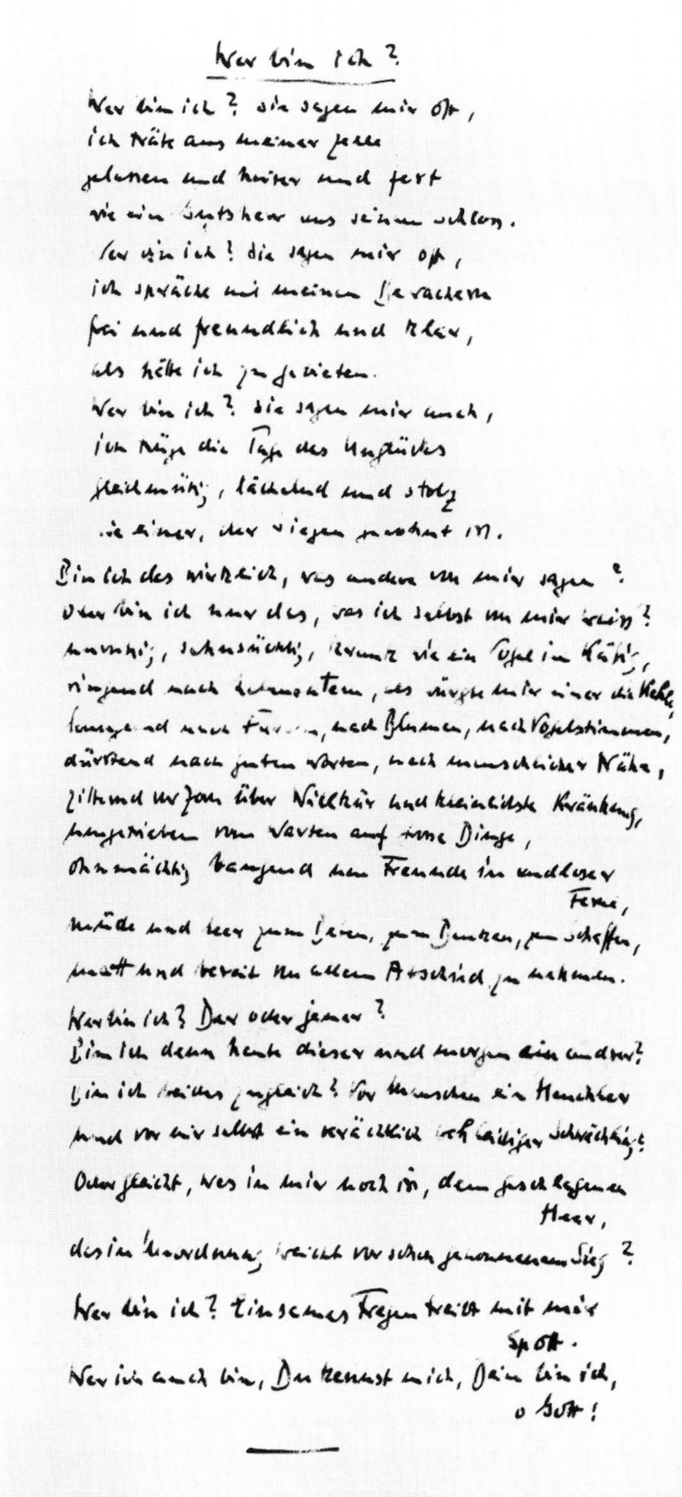

Wer bin ich?

Wer bin ich? Sie sagen mir oft,
ich träte aus meiner Zelle
gelassen und heiter und fest
wie ein Gutsherr aus seinem Schloß.
Wer bin ich? Sie sagen mir oft,
ich spräche mit meinen Bewachern
frei und freundlich und klar,
als hätte ich zu gebieten.
Wer bin ich? Sie sagen mir auch,
ich trüge die Tage des Unglücks
gleichmütig, lächelnd und stolz,
wie einer, der Siegen gewohnt ist.
Bin ich das wirklich, was andere von mir sagen?
Oder bin ich nur das, was ich selbst von mir weiß?
unruhig, sehnsüchtig, krank wie ein Vogel im Käfig,
ringend nach Lebensatem, als würgte mir einer die Kehle,
hungernd nach Farben, nach Blumen, nach Vogelstimmen,
dürstend nach guten Worten, nach menschlicher Nähe,
zitternd vor Zorn über Willkür und kleinlichste Kränkung,
umgetrieben vom Warten auf große Dinge,
ohnmächtig bangend um Freunde in endloser Ferne,
müde und leer zum Beten, zum Denken, zum Schaffen,
matt und bereit, von allem Abschied zu nehmen.
Wer bin ich? Der oder jener?
Bin ich denn heute dieser und morgen ein andrer?
Bin ich beides zugleich? Vor Menschen ein Heuchler
und vor mir selbst ein verächtlich wehleidiger Schwächling?
Oder gleicht, was in mir noch ist, dem geschlagenen Heer,
das in Unordnung weicht vor schon gewonnenem Sieg?
Wer bin ich? Einsames Fragen treibt mit mir Spott.
Wer ich auch bin, Du kennst mich, Dein bin ich, o Gott!

"Who am I?"
Handwritten original in ink, June 1944.

Who am I?

Who am I? They often tell me
I come out of my cell
serene and calm and steady
like a landowner coming out of his castle.
Who am I? They often tell me
I speak with my guards
in a free and friendly and clear way
as if it was I who had to give the orders.
Who am I? They often tell me
I endure the days of misery
equably, smiling, and proud
like one accustomed to victory.

Am I really what others say about me?
Or am I only what I know about myself? –
uneasy, full of longing, sick like a caged bird,
struggling to get my breath as if choking,
hungry for colors, for flowers, for birdsong,
thirsting for good words, for human closeness,
trembling with anger at arbitrary behavior, at the smallest offense,
driven by my expectation of great things,
powerlessly wondering about a joy infinitely far off,
tired and empty of strength to pray, to think, to work,
exhausted and ready to bid farewell to everything.
Who am I? This one or that one?
Am I this one today and someone else tomorrow?
Am I both at the same time? A hypocrite before other people and a contemptible sniveling weakling in my own eyes?
Or is my soul like a defeated army
retreating in chaos from a victory already won?

Who am I? I am the plaything of solitary questioning.
Whoever I am, you know me, I am yours, O God!

After the assassination attempt

On July 20, Klaus Bonhoeffer was on his way between the Bendler block and the houses in the Marienburger Allee. Was it still possible to hope? The army in Paris had stripped the SS of its power – would this have any effect on Germany? Klaus Bonhoeffer met Hans John and his brother Otto, who, by agreement with Stauffenberg, had attempted to make contact with the Allied headquarters, and had returned from Madrid on July 19.

On July 21, in the prison hospital, Dietrich Bonhoeffer heard on a foreign radio the news that the assassination attempt had failed. He was convinced that his fate was now sealed, and it was in this situation that he wrote the poem "Stations on the Way to Freedom."

On August 8, his uncle Paul von Hase was condemned to death by the People's Court and was executed in Plötzensee on the same day. His family was released from prison, but people avoided them for fear that contact might lead to their own imprisonment. The Schleicher family gave them a home.

On August 18, Hans John was arrested; his brother Otto managed to escape to Spain just in time. On August 22, Hans von Dohnanyi was transported to the concentration camp at Sachsenhausen. Dietrich resolved to flee, and Sergeant Knobloch, who had faithfully delivered his letters, declared himself ready to walk with the prisoner Bonhoeffer during the prison gate, ostensibly as part of his guard duties; the two of them would then lie low until they could make their escape. The family had already got hold of a boiler suit and food ration cards for Dietrich, but then Klaus Bonhoeffer was arrested on October 1, 1944, and Dietrich abandoned his plans, since they would only have meant an extra burden on his family.

Two days later, Rüdiger Schleicher was arrested in the Air Ministry. On October 5, the Gestapo also arrested Friedrich Justus Perels. On the same day, Dietrich wrote the poem "Jonah."

JONAH

They screamed at the prospect of death, and their
   bodies clawed
at the wet, storm-tossed ropes
and their eyes looked terror-stricken
at the sea in the chaos of suddenly unleashed forces.

"O eternal, good, enraged gods,
help or give a sign that would tell us
who has offended you with a secret sin,
the murderer or mocker forgetting his oath,

who has brought disaster on us by concealing his
   crime
for the sake of his wretched pride!"
Thus they prayed. And Jonah said: "I am the one!
I sinned before God. My life is lost.

Throw me overboard. The guilt is mine. God is very
   angry with me.
The pious is not to meet the same fate as the sinner!"
They trembled. But then with strong hands
they expelled the guilty one. And then the sea was still.

STATIONS ON THE WAY TO FREEDOM

Discipline.
If you leave home to seek freedom, learn above all
discipline of the senses and of your soul, so the desires
and your limbs will not lead you in many directions.
Let your spirit and your body be chaste, completely subject to you,
and obedient in seeking the goal laid down for it.
No one comes to know the mystery of freedom, except through discipline.

Deed.
To do and dare, not something arbitrary, but that which is right,
not floating in possibilities, but bravely taking hold of reality,
freedom is not in the flights of thought, but only in deed.
Emerge from timorous hesitation into the storm of events,
borne up only by God's commandment and your own faith,
and freedom will clothe your spirit exultantly.

Suffering.
A strange transformation: your strong, active hands
are bound. Powerless and solitary, you see the end
of your deed. Yet you breathe in relief and entrust that which is right
in silent comfort to a stronger hand: you are content.
Only for one instant, you touched freedom and were happy,
then you surrendered it to God, so that he might perfect it in glory.

Death.
Come now, you highest feast on the way to eternal freedom,
death, cast down the chains and walls that burden
our transitory body and our blinded soul,
that we may see at last what here we cannot see.
Freedom, we sought you so long in discipline, in deed, and in suffering.
Dying we recognize you now in God's face.

left page:

above left:
Hans John, assistant to Rüdiger
Schleicher at the Institute for
Aviation Law, University of
Berlin.

above right:
Otto John, who collaborated
with Klaus Bonhoeffer.

center:
On the patio of Dietrich's
parents' house, Marienburger
Allee. From left: Karl Bonhoeffer,
Paula Bonhoeffer, Renate with
Dietrich Bethge; behind them:
Ursula and Rüdiger Schleicher
(photograph taken July 1944).

below left:
Klaus Bonhoeffer.

below right:
Rüdiger Schleicher.

right page:

above left:
The SS occupy the Bendler block
on July 20. The executions were
carried out that night in front of
the sandpit to the left.

below left:
"Stations on the Way to Freedom," written on July 21, 1944,
one day after the failed assassination attempt.

above right:
Bonhoeffer's poem "Jonah,"
written after he abandoned his
escape plans, October 5, 1944.

The documents found at Zossen

At the end of September, in a branch of the Abwehr in Zossen, secret papers about the crimes of the National Socialists were discovered; they had been collected by Hans von Dohnanyi and they shed a surprising light on the extent and duration of the conspiracy. They prompted a new wave of arrests, and Dietrich's situation suddenly took a turn for the worse, since his real role now became clear. Besides this, all those who could have protected him were now themselves under arrest. When Hitler was informed about this material, he changed the original order for the speedy liquidation of the conspirators, and initiated an extensive investigation.

On October 8, Dietrich Bonhoeffer was moved from Tegel, the military prison for those awaiting trial, to Prinz-Albrecht-Straße, since the army was no longer responsible for prisoners connected with the failed assassination attempt. Bonhoeffer was able to take leave of his fellow inmates in Tegel: "It was already night, and the lights had been switched off, when Sergeant Linke opened the door of our cell. Dietrich did not want to leave the prison without first greeting his friends. He said 'Farewell!' and went to meet his fate" (Gaetano Latmiral).

Dietrich Bonhoeffer was in the dungeon of the National Security Office, Hans von Dohnanyi in Sachsenhausen concentration camp, Klaus Bonhoeffer, Rüdiger Schleicher, and Eberhard Bethge in the Gestapo prison on Lehrter Straße: this put an end to the various communication networks which had been built up between the prisons and the families outside, and between one cell and another. Nevertheless, a modest hope could surface even now, since all the prisoners were still accessible in prisons in Berlin. It was still possible for their families to do something for them.

At the end of December, in the dungeon of the Prinz-Albrecht-Straße, Dietrich wrote the poem "New Year" for Maria and for his mother's birthday on December 30. He managed to smuggle only three letters out of this prison, the last dated January 17, 1945.

Neujahr 1945.

von Dietrich Bonhoeffer
(Prinz-Albrecht-Strasse.)

Von guten Mächten treu und still umgeben,
behütet und getröstet wunderbar, –
So will ich diese Tage mit euch leben
und mit euch gehen in ein neues Jahr. –

Noch will das alte unsre Herzen quälen,
noch drückt uns böser Tage schwere Last,
Ach, Herr, gib unsern aufgescheuchten Seelen
das Heil, für das Du uns bereitet hast.

Und reichst Du uns den schweren Kelch, den bittern
des Leids, gefüllt bis an den höchsten Rand,
so nehmen wir ihn dankbar ohne Zittern
aus deiner guten und geliebten Hand.

Doch willst du uns noch einmal Freude schenken
an dieser Welt und ihrer Sonne Glanz,
dann woll'n wir des Vergangenen gedenken
und dann gehört dir unser Leben ganz.

Laß warm und still die Kerzen heute flammen,
die du in unsre Dunkelheit gebracht,
führ, wenn es sein kann, wieder uns zusammen.
Wir wissen es, Dein Licht scheint in der Nacht.

Wenn sich die Stille nun tief um uns breitet,
so lass uns hören jenen vollen Klang
der Welt, die unsichtbar sich um uns breitet,
all Deiner Kinder hohen Lobgesang.

Von guten Mächten wunderbar geborgen
erwarten wir getrost, was kommen mag.
Gott ist mit uns am Abend und am Morgen
und ganz gewiss an jedem neuen Tag. –

above:
Gestapo headquarters, Prinz-Albrecht-Straße, Berlin. The dungeon lay behind this façade.

below:
"New Year 1945": copy typed in 1945.

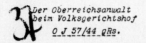

Der Oberreichsanwalt
beim Volksgerichtshof
O J 57/44 gRs.

Berlin, den 20. Dezember 1944.

Geheime Reichssach

H a f t !

A n k l a g e s c h r i f t

g e g e n

1.) den Chefsyndikus Dr. Klaus B o n h o e f f e r
aus Berlin-Grunewald, geboren am 5. Januar 1901
in Breslau, verheiratet,

2.) den ehemaligen Ministerialrat und Honorar-
professor Dr. Rüdiger S c h l e i c h e r aus
Berlin-Charlottenburg, geboren am 14. Januar 1895
in Stuttgart, verheiratet,

3.) den ehemaligen wissenschaftlichen Hilfsarbeiter
Dr. Hans J o h n aus Berlin-Dahlem, geboren am
31. August 1911 in Treysa b/Kassel, ledig,

4.) den Assessor Friedrich Justus P e r e l s
aus Berlin-Lichterfelde, geboren am 13. November
1910 in Berlin, jüdischen Mischling, verheiratet,

5.) den kaufmännischen Angestellten Dr. Hans
K l o ß aus Berlin, geboren am 28. November 1905
in Wien, jüdischen Mischling, verheiratet,
sämtlich zur Zeit auf Grund des Haftbefehls
des Ermittlungsrichters des Volksgerichts-
hofs in Berlin vom 20. Dezember 1944 in
Untersuchungshaft.

Gegen die Angeschuldigten erhebe ich die Anklage
wegen folgender Taten:
  Die Angeschuldigten Dr. Bonhoeffer und
Dr. Schleicher haben sich im Inlande in
den Jahren 1943/44 an dem vor dem ehemaligen Oberbürgermeister Dr. Goerdeler zusammen mit mutlos gewordenen Offizieren
und anderen Staatsfeinden betriebenen Unternehmen, unter Beseitigung des Führers
durch feigen Mord oder eine andere die
Möglichkeit seiner Tötung einschließende
Gewalttat das nationalsozialistische Re-
gime zu stürzen und den Krieg durch würde-
loses Paktieren mit den Feinden zu be-
enden, beteiligt und ihre Mitarbeit zuge-
sagt.
  Die Angeschuldigten Dr. John, Perels
und Dr. Kloß haben von den hoch- und lan-
desverräterischen Plänen der Verschwörer-
clique glaubhafte Kenntnis erlangt und
gleichwohl die ihnen obliegende Anzeige
dieses Vorhabens bei der zuständigen Be-
hörde unterlassen.

Interrogations, torture, executions

At the end of January, 1945, the special commissions under SS Commander Walter Huppenkothen, now head of the Abwehr (counter-espionage office), made a new attempt at progress in their investigations, and had Hans von Dohnanyi moved from Sachsenhausen to Prinz-Albrecht-Straße. On February 25, he succeeded in getting a secret message to his wife: "My weapon in this struggle is my illness ... The only solution is to gain time. I must make sure that it is impossible for them to interrogate me. The best thing would be a good dose of dysentery. It must surely be possible to get hold of a culture in the Koch Institute for medical purposes. If you cover a dish of food for me with a red cloth, and then put an ink-stain on the cup, I will know that it contains a really good infection." A further secret message, a few days later, confirms that he had received this "present": "You can hardly imagine how my heart beat when I saw a cup with a red cloth emerge from the bag ... The interrogations continue, and it is clear what awaits me, unless a miracle occurs." On April 6, 1945, Hans von Dohnanyi was executed in the concentration camp at Sachsenhausen.

above:
Accusation against Dr. Klaus Bonhoeffer, Prof. Dr Rüdiger Schleicher, Dr. Hans John, Assessor Friedrich Justus Perels, and Dr. Hans Kloss, December 20, 1944, addressed by the Attorney General to the People's Court.

below left:
Self-portrait by Hans von Dohnanyi, early in 1945, concentration camp, Sachsenhausen.

below right:
Secret message from Hans von Dohnanyi, February 25, 1945.

On February 2, 1945, Freisler pronounced the death sentence on Klaus Bonhoeffer and Rüdiger Schleicher. Eberhard Bethge, who was their fellow prisoner on Lehrter Straße, related after the War: "When I caught my father-in-law's eye and felt completely helpless in face of these events, he gave me a friendly wave and smiled so warmly that I was completely confused. Klaus greeted me by rising up with a scarcely perceptible shake of his shoulders, as if he wanted to show me how one must now behave." Klaus and Rüdiger were shot by the Gestapo on April 23.

In the afternoon of February 7, Dietrich disappeared from Berlin, and it proved impossible to get in touch with him. It was only several months later, thanks to an English radio station, that the survivors learnt how his life had ended.

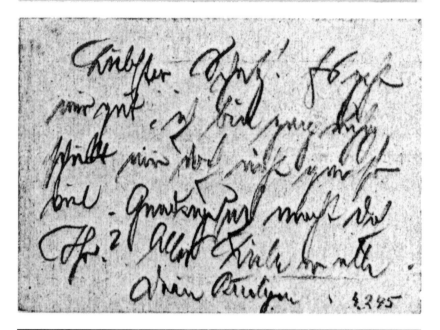

above:
Note sent by Klaus to Emmi Bonhoeffer, end of March 1945, from the prison on Lehrter Straße.

center:
Message from Rüdiger to Ursula Schleicher on the day after the death sentence was pronounced on himself and Klaus Bonhoeffer.

below:
A bomb crater in the Dorotheenstadt cemetery in Berlin was used as a mass grave. Those buried here included Klaus Bonhoeffer, Rüdiger Schleicher, Friedrich Justus Perels, and Hans John (photograph taken in 1945).

In recent years, I have learnt more and more the deeply this-worldly character of Christianity, and come to understand this. The Christian is not a "religious person," but quite simply a human being, just as Jesus – unlike John the Baptist, I would say – was a human being. What I mean is not the trivial this-worldliness of "enlightened," busy, comfortable, or lascivious persons, but the profound this-worldliness which is full of discipline and is continuously aware of death and resurrection. I believe that Luther lived in this kind of this-worldliness.

I remember a conversation with a young French pastor in America thirteen years ago. We had quite simply put the question what we wanted to do with our lives. He said: "I want to be a saint" (and I believe it possible that his wish was granted). At the time, this impressed me greatly. Nevertheless, I contradicted him and said, more or less: "I want to learn to believe." For a long time, I did not understand how deep this antithesis is.
I thought that I could learn to believe by trying to lead something like a holy life.

Later, I realized – and I have continued to realize this up to now – that it is only in the complete this-worldliness of life that one learns to believe.

May God lead us in his kindness through the course of time; but above all, may he lead us to himself.

From a letter written on July 21, 1944, one day after the failed assassination attempt on Hitler.

Flossenbürg
(1945)

In Berlin, Dietrich's parents attempted once again at the end of February to pick up his traces, writing to the prison on Prinz-Albrecht-Straße: "If it is possible, let us hear something from you soon." The letter was returned undelivered. No further messages for Dietrich were accepted there, and no information was given. Neither his family nor Maria von Wedemeyer, who searched for her fiancé in several camps, was told that he had already been deported to Buchenwald on February 7.

In the midday discussion in Hitler's headquarters on April 5, the decision was taken which resulted in Bonhoeffer's death. He was removed with other prisoners from Buchenwald and taken southwards. En route, on April 8, they celebrated the Sunday after Easter in the school at Schönberg, and Bonhoeffer was asked by the prisoners to hold a service. He preached on the text of the day: "By his wounds we are healed" (Isaiah 53:5), and spoke of the thoughts and decisions which captivity had brought to maturity in him. Then they had to move on – he just had time to pack his things and to write his name and address in large letters with a blunt pencil on the first and last and middle pages of his copy of Plutarch's texts. He left the book there, so that there would be some trace of him in the subsequent chaos; his brother Karl-Friedrich had given it to him while he was in the dungeon in Prinz-Albrecht-Straße. It was later discovered and was handed over to his family as his last message to them.

above:
Letter from Dietrich's parents, February 28, 1945.

center:
Texts by Plutarch, bearing Bonhoeffer's name and address.

below:
Administrative office and prisoners' quarters in the concentration camp, Flossenbürg.

"This is the end, for me the beginning of life"

The journey from Schönberg to Flossenbürg must have lasted until late in the evening. After a short trial, the SS court martial found Wilhelm Canaris, Hans Oster, Karl Sack, Ludwig Gehre, Theodor Strünck, Friedrich von Rabenau, and Dietrich Bonhoeffer guilty of high treason and sentenced them to death.

In the early hours of April 9, the executions were carried out. The SS doctor who was present noticed Bonhoeffer, without knowing who he was; ten years later, he wrote: "On the morning of that day, between 5 and 6 o'clock, the prisoners, including Admiral Canaris, General Oster ... and Judge Sack were led from the cells, and the verdicts of the court martial were read aloud. Through the half-open door in the barracks I saw Pastor Bonhoeffer kneeling, immersed in prayer to his God, before he took off his prison clothing. The devotion which was obvious in the prayer of this extraordinarily agreeable man, and his certainty that God heard him, made a very deep impression upon me. At the place of execution too, he uttered a brief prayer and then courageously and calmly mounted the ladder to the gallows. Death followed after a few seconds. In my activity as a doctor, which has lasted almost fifty years, I have never seen a man die with such devotion to God."

The last reported words of Dietrich Bonhoeffer were for Bishop Bell: "This is the end, for me the beginning of life."

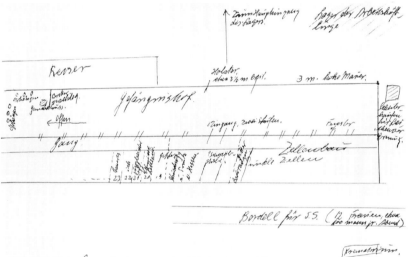

above:
Laundry in the concentration camp, Flossenbürg, where the SS court martial conducted its business.

center:
Barracks for special prisoners, drawn from memory by Colonel Hans M. Lünding, chief of the Danish Information Service, who occupied the cell next door to Admiral Canaris.

below:
Place of execution in the concentration camp, Flossenbürg.

It was only in July 1945 that his family were informed of Dietrich's death. They had switched on the English BBC station, as they often did, and they heard a memorial service for Dietrich at which his old friends, Bishop George Bell and Franz Hildebrandt, spoke.

In October, Dietrich's father wrote to his colleague, Prof. Jossmann, who had emigrated to Boston in the USA:

Dear colleague,

I was exceptionally delighted when your neighbors brought me greetings from you and I heard that things are going well with you in America and that your work is interesting. I know that you have heard that we have experienced terrible things, and have lost two sons (Dietrich, the theologian, and Klaus, the chief lawyer of Lufthansa) and two sons-in-law (Prof. Schleicher and Dohnanyi). You can readily imagine that this has left its mark on us old people. During all those years, we were anxious about those in prison, and those who were not yet in prison but were at risk. But since we were all agreed upon the necessity of acting, and my sons were also aware of what awaited them if the conspiracy should fail – and were ready to bid farewell to their own lives – we are sad indeed, yet also proud of their upright conduct ...

above:
Letter from Dietrich's father to
Prof. Jossmann in Boston,
October 8, 1945.

right page:

Dietrich's parents (photograph
taken after the War, 1945).

Note on photographic material and thanks.

The new edition of this book was possible only because numerous persons and institutions made available to the editors photographic material and documents for the first edition; much of this has been used here too.

We are abidingly grateful above all to the members of the Bonhoeffer family, especially to Mrs. Barbara Bayer née von Dohnanyi, Emmi Bonhoeffer, née Delbrück, Friedrich Bonhoeffer, Dorothee Bracher née Schleicher, Susanne Dress née Bonhoeffer, Klaus Delbrück, Kornelia van Eyck-Königs, Cornelie Grossmann née Bonhoeffer, Hans Christoph von Hase, Marianne Leibholz, Sabine Leibholz, Katharina Schmidt née Bonhoeffer, and Ruth Tafel.

We are also grateful to the following individuals (a = above; c = center; b = below; r = right; l = left):
Ruth-Alice von Bismarck, Munich (94 c., 94 b.); Irmgard Block, Berlin (108 a.l.); Keith Clements, Bristol (86 b.); Irmgard von Derschau, Asslar (108 a.r.); German Protestant parish in Sydenham and German Reformed parish of St Paul, London (72 c., 73 b., 75 b., 85 a.); Gudrun Diestel, Berlin (42 a.l.); Otto Dudzus, cologne (82 a., 82 b., 82 b., 83 r.); Heinz Fleischhack, Halle (109 b., 111 a., 111 b.); Jørgen Glenthøj, Borum (128 c., 128 b.); Helmut Gollwitzer, Berlin (97 a., 104 a.); Franz Hildebrandt, Edinburgh (63 c., 113 b.r.); Otto John, Hohenburg, Igl/Tirol (148 a.l., 148 a.r.); Otto Kasper, Singen (12); Werner Koch, Emlichheim (101 l.); Gaetano Latmiral, Naples (145 a.); Ruth Lindt-Koechlin, Berne-Ittingen (125 a.); Helga Perels, Kronberg (129 c.); Gottfried Rieger, Berlin (73 a.l.); Helle Sack, Offenbach (141 a.r.); Albrecht Schönherr, Waldesruh (53); Franz Schöttner, Markredwitz (156); Karl Stephan, Meisdorf/Harz (115 a., 120 a.); Rudolf Weckerling, Berlin (87 a.); Wolf-Dieter Zimmermann, Berlin (69, 100 b.).

The following archives have been very helpful to the editors (most names in German):
Stadtarchiv, Schwäbisch Hall (12, 13); Kunstamt Wilmersdorf, Berlin (30 c.); Walther-Rathenau-Oberschule, Berlin (31 b.); Stadtarchiv, Ulm (35 b.l.); Landesbildstelle, Berlin (39 c.r.); Bundesarchiv, Freiberg (64 a.l., 64 b.); Landesbildstelle, Berlin (65); Landeskirchlichesarchiv, Düsseldorf (66); Bildarchiv Preußischer Kulturbesitz, Berlin (72 a.; 80 a.l.); Landeskirchliches Archiv, Düsseldorf (85 b.); Evangelisches Zentralarchiv, Berlin (98 b.); Archbishop's Office, Uppsala (99 b.); Nordrheinwestfälisches Hauptstaatsarchiv, Düsseldorf (121 b.); World Council of Churches, Geneva (124 b.l.).

The editors and publisher are grateful to the following agencies for supplying photographic material:
Ullstein Bilderdienst, Berlin (60 a., 62 a.r., 62 a.l., 62 b.l., 79 b., 114 b.,123 a.r., 124 a.r., 124 b.r., 146 c., 146 b., 52 a., 131 a.l., 131 a.r., 132 a.l., 132 c., 133 b.); Süddeutscher Verlag Bilderdienst, Munich (61, 74 a., 75 c., 86 a., 150); Karl Barth Archiv, Basle (52 a., 66 a.); Gedänkstätte Deutscher Widerstand, Berlin (101 a.r.).

All texts by Bonhoeffer were translated by Brian McNeil from the edition of Dietrich Bonhoeffer's works in 17 volumes published by Chr. Kaiser Verlag/Gütersloher Verlagshaus, 1986-2002.